Praise for *What in the*

"This chronicle of one young reminder of the hope we have in Christ regardless of our external circumstances. Hannah offers encouragement, insight, and resources to help navigate the uncertainty of a cancer diagnosis with poise and a passion to bring glory to His name. I trust that Hannah's message of hope and courage will inspire you and anyone you know who is walking through a season of trials."

-**Joe White**, president, Kanakuk Kamps

"Hannah McGinnis faced her mortality head on when she received a diagnosis of cancer her senior year in college. This young woman's story of courage and faith in the face of a terrifying disease is an encouragement to any of us who are coping with inexplicable loss."

-**Peggy Wehmeyer**, former correspondent, ABC News

"When Hannah was diagnosed my first thought was, 'No way, not her!' But cancer attacks the young and robust as well as the old and infirm, and Hannah's book provides a thoughtful journey through the struggle. If you or someone young in your world has 'the Big C', this book will provide comfort and hope."

-**Pete Briscoe**, senior pastor, Bent Tree
Bible Fellowship, Carrollton, TX

"College and cancer are two words you typically do not expect to hear in the same sentence, much less expect to hear when describing a young, vibrant woman who has her whole life in front of her. When Hannah first received her diagnosis of cancer, she was a student at Wheaton College and certainly never anticipated this major turn in her journey. Through the help of family, friends, and faith she was able to walk through the challenge, growing, learning, and reaching out to others as a result. Her story is one of recovery, courage, and strength. I know you will be blessed from the life lessons Hannah learned along the road she had never planned for her life."

-**Karol Ladd**, author of *Thrive, Don't Simply Survive* and *The Power of a Positive Woman*

"God uses the trials of life as a classroom to teach us what it means to more fully surrender to Him. I for one am grateful that Hannah McGinnis decided to write down much of what God taught her in her battle with disease in *What in the World Are You Doing with Cancer?* Let her experiences and insights inspire and shape your story, whether you are facing cancer yourself, loving someone who is, or just stuck in the muck of life, whatever it may be."

-**Mark Saunders**, senior pastor, Bay Life Church, Brandon, FL

"Hannah McGinnis is the real deal. She honestly shares her journey through cancer with the strength of an athlete and the faith of a saint. Her story is not so much about her victory over the disease as it is about her trust in Jesus that is an example to any of us who face the realities of life. Follow her story with cancer. She can lead you to a deeper trust in God that will strengthen you through whatever you face today."

-**Gene Wilkes, Ph.D.**, senior pastor, Legacy Church, Plano, TX and author of *Jesus On Leadership* and *An Angel in the Flame*

"Hannah McGinnis invites us into the dark room of cancer that we dread to enter ourselves. This young woman—athlete, college student, and aspiring teacher—seeks a flu shot but discovers she must face the threat of a fatal disease. Her journey of grief and fear draws on strengths of perseverance, prayer, and the power of love from her family and her faith in God. The ultimate fight for life is the one we must wage in our own souls. Hannah's story will help you win it."

-**Dr. Gene Pond**, associate professor, Dallas Theological Seminary

What in the World Are You Doing with Cancer?

Facing the Unthinkable in the Prime of Life

Hannah McGinnis

WESTBOW
PRESS
A DIVISION OF THOMAS NELSON

WestBow Press books may be ordered through booksellers or by contacting:

WestBow Press
A Division of Thomas Nelson
1663 Liberty Drive
Bloomington, IN 47403
www.westbowpress.com
1-(866) 928-1240

Scripture quotations are from the Holy Bible: New International Version®. Copyright © 1973, 1978, 1984 by International Bible Society.

ISBN: 978-1-4908-0024-0 (sc)
ISBN: 978-1-4908-0025-7 (hc)
ISBN: 978-1-4908-0023-3 (e)

Library of Congress Control Number: 2013911895

Printed in the United States of America.

WestBow Press rev. date: 10/2/2013

on Christ the solid Rock I stand;
all other ground is sinking sand

For Mema

CONTENTS

FORWARD

As a parent of young children, I occasionally had terrifying thoughts of terrible things that could happen to my children, and every time I would shake the thoughts out of my head and admit that I didn't know how I could ever handle something awful happening to any of my three girls. However, always in the next breath, I would feel a sense of peace and assurance that, though I couldn't imagine how I could possibly handle any of those tragic scenarios, what I knew beyond a shadow of doubt was that God would meet me at my point of need and be everything I needed Him to be, if I would let Him.

Learning of my daughter Hannah's cancer diagnosis four years ago is exactly one of those moments I had envisioned so many years ago, and I am now a perfect example of God meeting me at my point of need and being everything I needed Him to be to walk through that unwanted journey. I was home alone when Hannah called from the mall to tell me that her doctor had called and confirmed the diagnosis of Hodgkin's lymphoma. All five family members were in different places when we learned of her cancer. I'm actually glad I was alone because it allowed me to process it more thoroughly than if we had all been together. With family, I know I would have immediately put my game face on and slipped into my mothering role of comforting and assuring the others that we could do this and everything was going to be okay. I'm a glass-half-full kind of person and tend to focus on the positives of most situations, but in that moment, I was having a hard time finding anything positive about Hannah having cancer. My first thoughts were, "No, I don't want to do this,"—not that I couldn't do it, but that I didn't want to. I remember taking a deep breath and saying, "Okay God, we're going to see if all the truths I've learned about You since I was a little girl are really true. I am going to trust You to be who I need You to be in this." By the time Hannah came home from the mall and Kevin got home from work, I was completely at peace—not necessarily that everything was going to work out the way I wanted it to, but I knew that God would be with me every step of the way, even if it ended badly.

Aside from learning the initial diagnosis, the next hardest thing I've ever had to do was to let Hannah go back to school and do all of her treatments in Chicago—instead of staying in Dallas where my husband and I could care for her. I remember wrestling with this possibility in my mind and "reminding" God that I was her mother and I was supposed to be the one to take care of her in such a time as this. I have never heard the audible voice of God, but I remember distinctly "hearing" Him in my mind remind me that while I was her mother, *He* was her Heavenly Father and that He loved her more than I could imagine, and that *He* would be the one orchestrating her care—and it might not even involve me! The picture I had in my mind is one where I had my fingers wrapped around Hannah's wrist and God gently prying each of my fingers off until I had completely let go. It was truly a moment of surrender. Although it seems absurd to say this, my thinking shows that for just a few selfish moments, I was acting as if this whole cancer journey was about *me*, instead of my daughter! Staying in Dallas for her treatments would have been the best plan for me, but it is so obvious that it was not the best plan for Hannah. This was the beginning of so many things God would teach me throughout her cancer. I realized about six weeks into it that "we were actually doing it"—that God really was meeting us at our every point of need. Seeing God's hand at work not only in Hannah's life but in mine, as well, caused me to even *thank* Him for her cancer about halfway through it because of all He was teaching us about complete trust in His sovereignty. I would have never imagined that going through my child's cancer would make me a better person, one more ready to completely surrender everything to God, but it definitely did. I know now that challenges such as cancer are about more than the physical battle. It is only one of many possible trials in which God wants to refine us and draw us closer to Him, and if we are willing to trust Him, it will be life changing. I am so thankful for Hannah's physical healing from Hodgkin's lymphoma, and I am equally thankful for the life changing spiritual lessons I learned because of her cancer.

Brenda McGinnis

I love the year-end holiday season. It is absolutely my favorite time of the year. It is a time to thoroughly enjoy the relationships that are the most important to you, to really give thanks for your blessings, and to pause for a brief moment from the crazy, busy world that you live in and enjoy all that the season offers. As this particular season approached, I remember telling my wife that we were really blessed and that although we had dealt with a lot of difficulties in life (the usual stuff—surgeries, financial pressures and difficulties, and typical family stresses and growing pains), we had not truly experienced any of the unthinkable pain and anguish that some people experience in life.

Days after that conversation, I was sitting in my office in Dallas, and Hannah called me from Chicago. She had just been to the health clinic on campus at Wheaton College to get a flu shot, and based upon a lump in her neck, the doctor wanted to know our family's history for cancer and recommended that she have an MRI of her neck. My predictable reaction was, *That's crazy because MRIs are expensive and college health clinics are clueless.* So I recommended that Hannah call some of her friends for a recommendation to go see a "real doctor." That week Hannah saw a "real doctor" who also immediately asked her what our family's history for cancer was and recommended an MRI.

And so it started. We were about to journey through the unthinkable pain that I had just discussed with my wife that we had never experienced. This journey into uncharted waters for us started with the initial uncertainty of the nature and extent of our daughter's cancer and wondering whether this was something that would kill her, end her life prematurely, or permanently damage her. It then continued with us watching over a protracted period of time as the doctors slowly poisoned her with chemotherapy—to the point where her body simply could not take it any longer—to kill the cancer cells in her body. We watched her hair fall out, her arms become scarred like an addict from all the needle marks, her skin turn pale and purple, and her general appearance look like the proverbial "death warmed over." We watched as her immune system was completely destroyed, knowing that even a simple infection could cause her to be immediately admitted to the hospital as a potentially life threatening situation. Through this process, we discovered that chemotherapy basically drains the life out of you.

In sociology, you learn that it is human nature to want to believe that people who suffer somehow are bad people. We simply don't want to believe that innocent people suffer. Somehow it makes us feel less vulnerable if the person who suffers is a bad character. In short, we want to think that they deserve it so we can rationalize that it never could happen to us. That's a big problem here. You don't know Hannah. Hannah is an angel. Respectful, thoughtful, compassionate, and innocent. Passionate about life and deep relationships. A loyal friend. College athlete and team player. Loves all things Disney. An absolute sweetheart. I visited her in her dorm room at Wheaton College when she was a freshman and asked her why she had twenty plus pictures and names of friends on her bulletin board. Hannah responded, "Daddy, those are the people that I pray for." That was Hannah being Hannah. Nobody gets off easy here. If this can happen to Hannah, it can happen to you or anybody that you love dearly.

This journey was the hardest thing we had ever dealt with as parents or as a family. When we knew she had cancer but didn't know the nature or extent of it, I remember closing my door at the office and weeping uncontrollably for the better part of three days. I was numb and worthless for most of the first couple of months. There is nothing worse as a parent than losing control of a situation and watching your child in pain. This journey was a show stopper for us. From our perspective as her parents, it was agonizingly painful and so inexplicably unfair. But this is Hannah's journey and her story. If you or somebody close to you is experiencing a journey like this, we hope that this book blesses and comforts you and gives you hope.

Kevin McGinnis

What in the World Are You Doing with Cancer?

Cancer. The "C word." It's not supposed to apply to you. You're in the prime of life, healthy, maybe an athlete, probably a student, not that crazy tanning mom, not a chain-smoker, and not supposed to deal with things like this. Cancer happens to old people, right? Not you. Not now.

Not me.

When I found out I had Hodgkin's lymphoma, I immediately looked for books and other relevant resources for my situation, but I couldn't find much. Cancer-related information and help for those in their late teens, twenties, and thirties are pretty slim pickings. There are many books and support groups for breast cancer, prostate cancer, and even childhood cancer patients, but there's not much out there for young adults who fall in between.

At twenty-one, I exceeded the age limits for children's resources like Locks of Love and the Make a Wish Foundation, and I wasn't really a child anyway. I was fully cognizant of what was happening to me, though I wished I could have lived in childlike ignorance, oblivious to the gravity of my situation. But I wasn't really an "adult" in the proper sense of the word, either. I didn't make many life-altering decisions, and I didn't have life figured out (but who does, really?). I just didn't feel mature enough to have to handle this. Cancer at any age is difficult. I'm not saying cancer is worse for young adults, but I *am* saying having cancer as a young adult presents unique challenges that have largely gone unaddressed.

Cancer, seriously? It's such a bizarre and surreal thing to be diagnosed with cancer—that terrible and ominous word looming in the void, affecting millions each year. And yet, who ever really thinks it will happen to him or her? Not me, for sure. At a time when I was trying to figure out who I was and what to do with my life, having cancer as a part of my identity never once crossed my mind. Cancer was something I knew about and saw in movies or heard old people talk about at family gatherings. I secretly feared it coming for me, but then I remembered I'm not very unique and don't really stand out, so surely I'd be exempt from something like that. My life was pretty normal, and while at times I thought that was lame, I figured it also meant I'd be able to sidestep something tragic or monumental like cancer.

I was a college senior, twenty-one years old, and a varsity NCAA athlete in great health. I felt fine on the day I found out I had cancer. I didn't smoke, drink, do drugs, sleep around, go to tanning salons, or live an extraordinary life. And I'm pretty sure I've never been exposed to Agent Orange (yep, that's a risk factor for Hodgkin's). I'm actually a very ordinary person who makes safe choices. To many, being twenty-one means partying and living carefree, but my twenty-first year was one I'll never forget and that will impact me for the rest of my life for very different reasons. Instead of celebrating freedom, blowing off college classes, and being otherwise irresponsible, my twenty-first year included frequent trips to the hospital, learning what chemotherapy was, worrying about my white blood cell counts, listening to my body's limits, and wondering what on earth I was doing with cancer.

As I take you through my journey, I hope you understand a little more about what the big scary "C word" means physically, emotionally, and spiritually. My story is just one of millions, and I realize this work is not comprehensive. With so many different types and stages of cancer out there, I wouldn't purport it to be. But hopefully you can resonate with the feelings, fears, frustrations, and even joys I encountered along the way. I'll walk you through my journey, from the tests leading up to my diagnosis to my last treatment and where I went from there. Each chapter begins with an excerpt from the blog I wrote while I had cancer to give you a glimpse of how I felt amidst the crisis. Then I fill in the gaps, retelling my story and adding things that helped me along the way, things I wish I'd known or done, and things I've since learned.

I recently heard a pastor define encouragement as putting courage into someone. I love that because I love encouragement, and that's one of my two goals here. First, I hope to put courage into you, whether you have cancer, you know someone with cancer, or you're facing your own seemingly insurmountable struggle.

My second and most important goal is that you see Jesus Christ and the incredible ways God provided for and moved in my life when I had cancer. I want you to know, as the Israelites knew, that even when the sea towers above, an opposing army threatens, safety and the days of old beckon, and the way is physically impossible, in the words of author Robert J. Morgan, "The same God who led you in will lead you out."

CHAPTER 1

The Call

Wednesday, November 26, 2008

"He will have no fear of bad news; his heart is steadfast, trusting in the LORD" (Psalm 112:7).

So many thoughts are running through me right now—everything from uncertainty to trust; from frustration to knowing I am so incredibly blessed; from having so much to say to being at a loss for words.

Let me back up by saying I wanted to start this blog so as to not merit my parents' anger when they see the phone bill and realize I've way exceeded my text messaging limit. Also, let me take a moment to thank each and every person who has texted, called, emailed, and sent me a message to offer words of wisdom, encouragement, support, and prayer. I have been brought to tears more times than you can imagine. In fact, most of the times I've cried so far have been from knowing God has blessed me with incredible family and friends. Y'all have already been a huge support system, and that has made a world of difference.

On to what we know: I got a call this morning from one of the first doctors I saw in Wheaton—who happens to be a Christian and has been praying for me—and he talked to the pathologist this morning. I officially now know what the biopsy showed: I have Hodgkin's lymphoma. While the fact that I have cancer in and of itself sucks, the doctor told me if I have to have any kind of cancer, Hodgkin's is the kind I want, apparently. He said it's very treatable, so praise the Lord! The other good news is that I still have no symptoms (other than a hole and imminent scar in my neck from the biopsy)—no weight loss, night sweats, fever, or fatigue—and the doctors don't think the cancer has spread to my lungs or anywhere else yet, so they think we caught it pretty early.

While we now know what's going on with me, we haven't figured out what treatment to have, where to have it (Chicago or Dallas), which doctor to see, etc. My family and I would *love* your prayers for wisdom and continued peace as we sort this out. As for me, I'm honestly doing okay—at least for now. I can't promise it will always be like that, but I am doing great right now. There are a couple of things in the back of my mind helping me out at the moment.

First, I've had enough injuries (two requiring surgery and one requiring stitches in the past three years) to know that "Why?" is not the question to ask God. This year I dislocated my kneecap during a conference match of my final season of volleyball. It was frustrating to have poured so much heart and hard work into the season to then miss half of conference, coming back for the last two weeks and clearly not at my top ability. As much as each injury was disheartening and I wondered why I had to keep facing the same obstacles and re-learning old lessons, maybe the reason for all of them was to collectively prepare me to deal with this substantial disease.

Secondly, as so many have reassured me, God is in control and nothing is out of His hands. I've been learning over the past couple of months that God is *good*, not out to get me. He is the Rock we cling to, and He is faithful. Give thanks that He is sovereign.

As we find out more info about where and when treatment will happen, I'll make sure to update y'all. In the meantime, I think my family is taking this the hardest, so I'd love prayer for them, for miraculous healing, for wisdom as we sort out details, and for "the peace that passes all understanding" (Philippians 4:7). Thank you, thank you, thank you for all of your love and prayers.

On Christ the solid Rock I stand,

Hannah
Posted at 1:43 p.m.

Standing inside a store at NorthPark Center mall on the morning of Wednesday, November 26th, I tried to enjoy the distraction of shopping with Caroline, one of my best friends. It was the day before Thanksgiving, and I was home from Wheaton College (near Chicago) spending time with my family in Dallas. Buried inside my purse, my iPhone started ringing, and I scrambled to find it while I stepped outside to answer the call. The name "Dr. Santi" appeared on the screen, and my heart skipped a beat. I knew the gravity and potential impact of this call for me, my family and friends, and my future.

I had just spent the better part of the last month enduring a myriad of tests and doctors' appointments, including a surgical excision of a chunk of my neck. Reading between the lines from my doctors' visits and procedures, I knew there was a good chance I had some form of cancer. The range of types and severity of cancer was wide and the life-changing—or even ending—implications scary. This was the call we were all waiting for and dreading.

As I slid my finger across my phone to answer it, I knew I was about to enter deeper into an already surreal experience. On the other end of the line, Dr. Santi began to explain that it was not his practice to call patients out of office, but since he knew I was home with my family, he wanted to call so we could figure out "important decisions" while we were all together. At that moment, he confirmed my worst fears. I knew whatever he was about to say couldn't be good. No one has to make "decisions" if life's flowing smoothly. Suddenly I stepped into a whole new reality—an unthinkable one that somehow included cancer.

Dr. Santi proceeded to explain what the previous month's tests and lymph node biopsy revealed: I had Hodgkin's lymphoma, the nodular sclerosing type, and he thought it was stage IIA. Having no idea what that meant, but knowing my parents would want to know exactly what he said, I dug out a pen from my purse and, for lack of finding something better to write on, scribbled down the information on the edge of my Nordstrom shopping bag. What a surreal way to find out I had cancer. Other shoppers ambled on their way, passing me by, while my world suddenly froze. When people ask me what it was like to get the news, I can only say it was bizarre and I'm really grateful Nordstrom used white shopping bags with ample writing space that season.

Dr. Santi reassured me that my diagnosis was good because around 85% of Hodgkin's patients beat the disease, and since we had caught it so early, I had a great outlook. Having followed my progression of tests for weeks, Dr. Santi was concerned for me personally. He advised me to stay home in Dallas to complete treatment so that I would have my family nearby to support and care for me. He reassured me that he and his wife were praying for me, and we hung up as I tried to process what I'd just heard.

Watching me from inside the store, Caroline read from my expression that the conversation had been difficult. She came outside, gave me a big hug, and asked what the doctor said. As I repeated the details, I started to cry for only the second time in my whole journey to the diagnosis. Strangely, my tears were not out of fear, anger, or sadness at the news; they came when I told Caroline that my doctor advised me to stay home from school, which meant withdrawing from Wheaton in the middle of my senior year of college with only one semester to go.

It's funny how, in the middle of mind-blowing moments, the things we focus on can be such a small part of the equation. I think God in His grace allows us to process crazy times by swallowing things one bit at a time, so we're never fully able to comprehend or worry about the whole picture. In *A Million Miles in a Thousand Years*, Donald Miller writes,

"After a tragedy, I think God gives us a period of numbing as a kind of grace. Perhaps He knows our small minds, given so easily to false hope, couldn't handle the full brunt of reality."[11] I think sometimes during trials that same numbing occurs. That's what I experienced upon finding out I had cancer. Was I concerned that I might die? Nope. Somehow I, an average student, cared most about school.

I called my parents from the mall and told them the news, and afterward Caroline and I promptly said goodbye, and I drove home.

A YEAR OF RISKS

To understand my tears at the thought of leaving Wheaton, I should also tell you more of my history there and the journey leading up to that fateful November day.

I arrived at Wheaton College for volleyball two-a-days before my freshman year started, not overly excited to be there. Wheaton was my default school because I didn't get into my number one choice. I was so sure I'd get into my first choice that when the rejection letter came, I went into shock for a time. I'd heard that a good rule of thumb for picking colleges was to choose the best school you got into, so of the other three schools I'd reluctantly applied to (since I knew I was going to get into my first choice, of course), Wheaton was by far the best academically. I accepted my plight, but unlike most of my excited high school classmates, when summer waned and it came time to pack up and move off to college, I went about things mechanically, resigned to my fate.

Because I had such low expectations, Wheaton exceeded all of them and more, and I had an absolute blast my freshman year. I made great friends, I was a starting player on the volleyball team, I was spontaneous and somewhat irresponsible, and I enjoyed my independence. It was the most fun I'd had in a long time.

As great as my first year was, my sophomore year was that bad. Some liked to call it the "sophomore slump" but I thought that was too kind; I renamed it the "sophomore suck." I had shoulder surgery on a volleyball injury that occurred in the spring and worsened over the summer, so I redshirted, sitting out my sophomore season of volleyball. I felt pain most of the year, sat bored to tears on the sidelines during practice, and watched helplessly as my teammates struggled with a lack of heart.

Outside of volleyball, I couldn't sleep at night because of the steady ache from knots running across my shoulders. I would lie awake until 3 a.m., exhausted, but still unable to sleep. My physical therapist told me I needed to relax, and I responded in frustration, "I *am* relaxed!" to which she laughed and shook her head. My tension only added to my insomnia. Academically, I took three upper-level literature classes, so I spent four hours reading and studying in the library every night. On top of all that, some of my closest relationships from my freshman year were changing, and I felt like my equilibrium was off, like I couldn't succeed or hold on to anything. I considered transferring, quitting volleyball, and studying abroad just to change things up—anything to ignore the fact that God wanted me at Wheaton.

My junior year brought a change in the tide. In church after my first week back at school, I finally came to terms with the fact that God had a purpose for me at Wheaton. I surrendered to it, deciding I would get excited about where I was. It was a year of risks as I confronted my fears, both big and small. Despite my fear of heights, I climbed a tin roof that any moment might crash to the ground below so that I could paint over graffiti on a mission trip. I ate lamb which, for a picky eater like me, was a huge deal. I finally told a guy how I felt about him face to face, and though I didn't receive a word in response, I felt on top of the world, as if I could do anything. I decided holding on to fear ultimately said God wasn't big enough to handle the situation. By letting go, I learned about fully trusting God to be faithful, even in minor ways.

Senior year was mostly great because I was having fun, soaking up the experience. Volleyball was disappointing because of my knee injury and some conflict between other players, but off the court I built great relationships with my teammates. Though the fall had been a struggle in many ways, I knew my character had grown, and I felt sure that the rest of my time at Wheaton could only be smooth sailing. Leaving at this point—down to my final semester of college—was such a defeating prospect. To have come so far, from whining about God's plan to finally getting on board with it and enjoying where I was, only to have to quit *so* close to the finish line did me in. I had finally made peace with where I was, and I did *not* want to leave.

Thus, the tears came. It's funny to think about what pushed me over the edge—not the barrage of medical tests I went through, nor the scary prospect of cancer, nor even the confirmed diagnosis, but not finishing college on time mattered most. That's how we are when we're young, though. We don't have time to worry about cancer and we can't be bothered with the threat of death because we're too busy enjoying life, pursuing our plans, and trying to change the world.

SOMETHING IS NOT RIGHT

People often ask me how I first knew something was wrong, and I'm taken back to the fall of 2008. Sometime during volleyball practice (apparently I was a bit distracted), I noticed a swollen lymph node above my collar bone on the left side of my neck. I figured I was about to get sick or something, so I just kind of blew it off. Then, during our Homecoming game in early October, I dislocated my kneecap, so all of my focus shifted to rehab and getting back on the court. At that point, I had a month left of my senior volleyball season, and we were in the thick of conference matches, so I was single-minded in getting back to play as quickly as possible.

With my focus on rehab, the lymph node would have to wait—even when one multiplied into two. One day in the athletic training room, I mentioned the nodes to my trainer Kirsten Fumagalli. She said they weren't normal and I should monitor them to see if they grew, so I did, but I had bigger issues to tackle at the time. Over the course of October, I kept an eye on the nodes and observed that they were getting bigger, but I hadn't come down with a cold or any other sickness I figured they signaled. Two weeks after my injury, I returned to the volleyball court with a throbbing and swollen knee but greatly determined spirit. I finished out the final two weeks of my volleyball career that way, and my twelve years as "Hannah the volleyball player" ended in a playoff loss on Tuesday, November 4th.

With my season and career officially over, I decided I should get a flu shot. I got one every year, but since it made my arm sore, I always waited until volleyball season ended. I mean, I was already fighting knee pain, so why add a sore arm to the mix? That Friday, I went into the Wheaton College Health Center for my flu shot, and when the nurses asked if I was sick before administering the shot, I said no. Then I added that I had a couple of swollen lymph nodes above my collar bone, so I'd been wondering if I was "secretly sick," even though I felt fine. The nurses cleared me to get the shot, but upon further inspection, they told me I needed to go to the emergency room and undergo a computerized tomography (CT) scan and an X-ray, and they asked me about my family's history with cancer.

I left the health center semi-alarmed but mostly skeptical, so I immediately called my dad. You see, seven months earlier during the spring, I was putting up the volleyball net before practice, raising the pole to its correct height. The pole had a broken piece, and as I slid the pole into its place in the gym floor, the top of it came crashing down to the base with my hand caught in between. I pulled my hand out and immediately saw blood and a v-shaped chunk of skin missing from the palm of my right hitting hand. I called my teammate Emily over, said, "Tell Coach I'm probably gonna miss practice," and ran to the athletic training room.

The trainers looked at my wound and said they normally stitched up injuries, but the hand was too dangerous for them, so they sent me to our college health center. The health center said the same thing, so they drove me to the ER where I received ten stitches and knew the rest of my spring season was over. A few weeks later, my dad got the ER bill, and after we recovered from our five thousand dollar shock, my dad enforced a new rule: I must call him before going to the ER (though I'm not sure how that works if I'm unconscious or something). So, as I left our health center seven months later, like a good daughter, I called my dad.

I began, "Hey, I just left the health center for my flu shot, and when they saw my swollen lymph nodes, they gave me a prescription for an X-ray and CT scan at the ER."

Confused, my dad replied, "What? What lymph nodes? What are you talking about? Have these even been a problem? Do you even feel sick? Go see a real doctor!"

I agreed with his assessment since it seemed like the health center freaked out about nothing. I talked to my teammate Ruth's parents, Lynda and Rick Armstrong, who lived in the city of Wheaton, and they referred me to their local physician. However, he was fully booked, so his office referred me to a Dr. Chris Santi, someone I'd never met and who was now a referral from a referral from a friend. On Monday, November 10th, I met Dr. Santi, and he asked about my symptoms. Then he asked if I had a history of cancer in my family, now the second time I'd been asked that question. I hoped that was standard procedure—I mean, I was in a doctor's office; they ask sweeping questions like that, right?

Dr. Santi asked if I went to Wheaton and I said yes and that I played volleyball. He smiled and explained he'd played volleyball in college and that his wife graduated from Wheaton. He then explained that my lymph nodes could be nothing, but they also could be something, so he wanted me to see an ear, nose, and throat (ENT) specialist that week. Dr. Santi told me he'd be praying for me, and whatever the outcome, I shouldn't worry because God is the ultimate healer and has perfect plans.

I'm so grateful for him and how the Lord led me to a godly doctor, and I appreciated his encouragement—God *is* the ultimate healer and we're in His hands. But at the same time, his words made me think, *Wait a second. If he's telling me not to worry, that means it's normal if I do? Great. I wasn't concerned before, but now I am.* Anxiety hit me for the first time, but I tried to suppress my simmering fear by recalling his encouragement and remembering I was a very ordinary person, so things like cancer didn't happen to people like me.

I saw the ENT on Friday, and after checking things out, he scheduled a CT scan to determine whether I'd need a biopsy or not. Now, when you hear the word "biopsy," only one thing comes to mind. Biopsies can be negative and show that there's no problem, but regardless of the results, the word "biopsy" is intrinsically linked with "cancer." When the ENT mentioned the word, I realized Dr. Santi hadn't been kidding. This really could *be* something—and something more than a simple infection.

This could be cancer.

EARLY SIGNS OF GOD'S PROVISION

We scheduled my CT scan for Wednesday, November 19th, and in the meantime, I attended my regularly scheduled classes and chapels at Wheaton. Two days before my appointment, a professor named Dr. Hill spoke in chapel about receiving the Lord's comfort during a difficult time in his family. At the end of his talk, he said there would be people outside distributing cards with Bible verses that had helped him walk through that trial. I grabbed a card on my way out the door. Descending the steps of Edman Chapel, I glanced down and noticed one of my favorite verses written on it, one I'd come to cling to in rough situations before, and one that proved perfect for my present anxiety: "But now, this is what the

Lord says—He who created you, O Jacob, He who formed you, O Israel: 'Fear not, for I have redeemed you. I have summoned you by name; you are Mine'" (Isaiah 43:1).

The passage goes on in verses two and three to say, "When you pass through the waters, I will be with you; and when you pass through the rivers, they will not sweep over you. When you walk through the fire, you will not be burned; the flames will not set you ablaze. For I am the Lord, your God, the Holy One of Israel, your Savior."

We sing a song based on that verse at Kanakuk, the Christian summer camp in Missouri I went to and worked at for fifteen summers. I'd been singing the words over and over to myself during the month of November, so when I saw that card, I got chills. Relief and peace overwhelmed me all at once, and I felt like God was affirming His presence.

Fear not. I repeated those words to myself remembering that when we pass through the raging storms, the rushing waters, and the burning fire, God will bring us out intact. I'm always struck by the wording of those verses: they say *when* rather than *if* we pass through those times. Though we like to think we're invincible, we all walk through difficulties in life, and *when* they arrive we can remember that the Lord has redeemed us, so we need not fear.

I slipped the card into my wallet, and it remains there to this day. What perfect comfort when I so needed a reminder that God was still in control.

I had my CT scan on Wednesday and nervously awaited the results. On Friday, I was at a basketball game with my teammates Stef and Kelli when the ENT called. I gave the girls a knowing look, so they stepped into the hallway with me. The doctor told me the results from the CT scan showed something concerning, so I needed a biopsy—soon. Suddenly fear set in, and I'm so grateful Stef and Kelli were there. They hugged me, reassuring me that they were praying and would help with anything. I called my parents and passed on the update, and since "biopsy" conjured up the same fear of cancer in their minds as in mine, my mom decided to fly up and join me for the procedure.

On Monday morning, I attended my Drugs and Society class, and my friend Maggie, noticing I seemed out of sorts and knowing I'd been through many appointments, told me she was praying for me. I couldn't contain my tears any longer. For the first time in this journey, I broke down as Maggie hugged me. She prayed for me, letting me know she would help and that God was sovereign. I still remember that moment so vividly because I'd been trying so hard to hold it together, but suddenly I couldn't anymore. Finally I acknowledged my suppressed fears, and I lost it. Thankfully, I did manage to recover enough to sit through class and then chapel. After chapel ended, I went to my house and waited for Mrs. Armstrong to pick me up and take me to the hospital.

THE BIOPSY

There are different types of lymph node biopsies. In one, the doctors take a needle and remove some cells from the node, but in the other, they actually surgically remove the node. A new ENT took charge of my biopsy, and she said the needle type was less invasive but less conclusive, so she recommended the full node removal. However, she cautioned, I'd have a scar on my neck that would show in the future when I wore formal dresses, so it was my choice. It took all of my restraint not to sarcastically quip, *Yeah, I would rather chance missing a cancer diagnosis than have a scar for the countless formal events I get invited to. Thanks for the heads-up. You know me so well.* Instead, I remembered my manners and politely said that with cancer on my mind, I'm pretty sure that was the last thing I cared about, so I opted for the full removal.

My teammate Jamie's mom had picked my mom up from the airport, and they arrived with about ten minutes to spare before I met with the anesthesiologist. Soon, I was heading back to the operating room. After I got out of surgery, I still felt foggy when the ENT came by. She said the initial tests showed that my lymph node looked "suspicious of lymphoma." *Suspicious of lymphoma? Why don't you just call a spade a spade and tell me I have cancer,* I wanted to snap back. She said it would take a couple of days to definitively process the biopsy, so I should wait for a call to come back in. Because Thursday was Thanksgiving, my mom and I had a flight home to Dallas the next day. We didn't want to wait a full week to come back and hear the results in office, but there was nothing we could do. The ENT left the room, and a nurse came in to follow up with us. My mom recently told me that the nurse said Aaron's benediction from Numbers 6:24-26 over me. In this passage, God gives Moses instructions for how the priest Aaron and his sons are to bless the Israelites. The nurse recited, "[24]The Lord bless you and keep you; [25]the Lord make His face shine on you and be gracious to you; [26]the Lord turn His face toward you and give you peace." Maybe my anesthetic was still going strong at that point, or maybe the fact that I'd just been told I had a good shot at cancer kept me from hearing her words, but for whatever reason, I have no recollection of that moment. To my mom, however, it was a striking reminder of God putting people in our paths to encourage us. And in hindsight, hearing about her benediction was yet another reminder to me that God was protecting me and had gone before me from the very start of my trip through cancer. After she finished up, we left the hospital, spent the night at the Armstrongs' house, and flew home the next day.

That's why when Dr. Santi called me on my cell phone the day before Thanksgiving, though it was unconventional to break such weighty news over the phone—especially given my location at the mall—I'm so thankful he made my situation a priority. I hadn't even seen him since my November 10th appointment—my only face-to-face encounter with him to this day—but his connection to Wheaton, volleyball, and the Lord led him to stay involved in my case. He'd called the ENT's office to check on my status, and when the hospital staff said it wasn't their practice to call patients out of office with such significant results, Dr. Santi took it upon himself to deliver the news because he knew I was home with my family. Praise the Lord for placing us in exactly the right place at exactly the right time! Dr. Santi was truly a godsend, one of many early signs that God had already gone ahead to prepare the way for what was (to me) an unplanned journey.

THE JOURNEY BEGINS

On the morning of my biopsy, I sat in chapel, my mind wandering (what with the impending surgery a couple hours later and all), but I did at least pay attention during the closing prayer. As I listened to the prayer requests, I heard about a girl named Kirsten Friedl who had her final chemotherapy treatment on Tuesday, two days before Thanksgiving. During the middle of the prayer, I got out my iPhone and typed her name in my notes. I'm not sure why, other than the Holy Spirit prompted me, but I remember thinking, *Hmmm...we're praying for this girl who has cancer, and I'm getting a biopsy. She might be someone I'll want to talk to later.* I still have that note saved in my phone, dated 11/24/2008.

On Wednesday, two hours before I met Caroline at the mall to go on our infamous shopping trip, I sat waiting in my orthopedic doctor's office to discuss my knee injury. Flipping through the notes in my phone, I saw the one with Kirsten's name. I figured since cancer was likely in the picture, I would send her a Facebook message to find out a little more info. I wrote:

> Wednesday, November 26, 2008
>
> Hey Kirsten—I realize you don't know me, but I heard your name on Monday as we were praying for you in chapel. I hope all is going well and that your treatment has been successful. I actually just had a lymph node biopsy on Monday and the early tests showed that it was "very suspicious" of lymphoma. In that, I wanted to let you know I'm praying for you and would ask if you could do the same for me. I've obviously never been down this road before, but I know God is so faithful. Sorry if this throws you off, but your name was on my heart after

chapel prayer. I hope and pray you have a blessed Thanksgiving and that you are doing great.

God bless,

Hannah McGinnis

I sent the message and figured she'd either think I was a creepy stalker or some random girl freaking out about something trivial in contrast with her cancer. However, Kirsten responded quickly and sweetly.

Wednesday, November 26, 2008

Hey Hannah! I'm so glad you messaged me! It definitely doesn't throw me off; I actually did the same to another Wheaton student who was recently diagnosed with cancer and I wanted to talk to her and see how she was doing. So no worries.

I was diagnosed with Hodgkin's lymphoma at the end of May, and for about a month afterward it was crazy with all the tests and doctors' appointments. I started chemo towards the end of June and after just the four chemos, I had a PET scan and it was clear. Unfortunately after that, I still needed to finish up my last eight chemos, but the good news is I didn't need radiation. So since then, I've been going downtown [to Chicago] for chemo every other week, and I actually just had my last one yesterday! So I'm really excited about being done, and hopefully my PET scan at the beginning of January will also be clear. So that's a little bit of my story.

I'll definitely pray for you. I know it's a scary time for you, especially not knowing what's ahead. Please trust God. His strength is made perfect in our weakness. I've definitely learned a ton throughout these times. Please keep me updated with what goes on, and thanks for messaging me.

I'm not sure if you're going to be around Wheaton anymore or not, but if you are, I'd love to get together for a meal or something.

Praying for you,

Kirsten

Right after I received her message, my orthopedic doctor came into the room, so I couldn't respond right away. He and I discussed my kneecap and why it didn't like to stay in place. When I told him I was waiting to hear back about whether I had cancer or not, he said I'd need to wait for those results before moving ahead with knee surgery. Then he added that he had two children: a daughter who was a former Kanakuk camper of mine and a son who had passed away from cancer years before. He said he knew what I faced, he would pass on my prayer request to his daughter, and his family would be praying for me. Once again, right when I needed it, God placed people in my path to encourage me.

I left his office and headed for the mall where I met Caroline and got Dr. Santi's cancer call. After I drove home—in shock most of the way—I sat down with my parents to rehash what we knew. We then headed into my dad's study to make some calls. First my dad dialed up Dr. Santi to confirm the news. Dr. Santi repeated what he'd told me, assuring my parents that, though having cancer was unfortunate, I'd at least contracted a "good kind" compared to other types. He said I would need to get more tests and scans completed before starting treatment, and he added that we should act as quickly as possible. Typically, Dr. Santi explained, Hodgkin's patients went through four rounds of chemo followed by radiation, and he knew some oncologists I could see in the Wheaton area if, indeed, I decided to stay in Illinois. Vowing to help us in any way possible, he hung up after reminding us that God was in control.

I remembered Kirsten had responded to my message earlier but I'd left her hanging. After her first message, I did a little Facebook research and found out she was a sophomore who played tennis at Wheaton. She'd grown up around Wheaton and actually went to school with the Armstrongs' daughters. I quickly sent her a response.

Wednesday, November 26, 2008

Kirsten,

Thanks so much for your response. Congrats on (hopefully!) finishing your last round of chemo. I actually found out between my morning message and now that I, too, have Hodgkin's lymphoma (nodular sclerosing kind), which is I guess cool because it's so rare, so you and I together make up 2/3000 women who get it each year. Thanks though, seriously, for your words of wisdom—I'm sure it would have been nice for you to have someone go ahead of you (which it sounds like you may have), but thank you for offering encouragement already.

We're now trying to figure out where to do treatment—at home in Dallas or back at school—and my preference would be at school so I can finish up since I only have this semester and then five hours in the spring, but I'd love prayer for wisdom on that in the meantime. And, if I'm back at Wheaton, I would love to get a meal.

So that I don't have to keep texting my whole friend and family system, I started a blog, so maybe you can check that out.

I hope you and your family have a blessed Thanksgiving, and I might be asking some questions as we get around to treatment and such. Know that I will continue to pray the chemo did its job for you, and I'd love your updates as well.

In Him,

Hannah

Kirsten replied with her phone number in case I wanted to ask questions, talk through things with someone who understood, or have her mom reassure my parents. I called to do all three. My dad put the call on speakerphone, and we heard from Kirsten and then her mom. Kirsten explained the road to her diagnosis. She'd gone in to the health center in January of 2008 with swollen lymph nodes above her collarbone, but the nurses and doctors ran some tests and put her on antibiotics, thinking it was some sort of infection. After a few months when the swelling persisted, she went back to the center, and they concluded that she should take different antibiotics. It wasn't until May that Kirsten had a more definite CT scan showing she had something much bigger than an infection.

Suddenly, I understood why the nurses and doctor in our college health center freaked out and told me to go to the ER on my first visit in November. When I called my dad, we scoffed and thought, *Oh, they're just a college health center. What do they* really *know?* Come to find out, they had been exactly right. Their panic at my lymph nodes was because only six months earlier, they'd misdiagnosed the same exact kind of cancer, and they weren't making that mistake again. The moral of that anecdote is: never underestimate your college health center.

Kirsten started chemotherapy right after classes ended in May and had just finished her twelfth and final treatment the day before our conference call. What a small world: two female athletes at tiny Wheaton College got the exact same type and stage of a semi-rare cancer.

Kirsten raved about her doctor and nurses. She praised Dr. Leo Gordon, a teaching oncologist at Northwestern Memorial Hospital in downtown Chicago. Though the commute through traffic was further than completing treatment closer to the city of Wheaton, Kirsten said it was worth it. She loved that, while other oncologists prescribed four rounds of chemo followed by radiation, Dr. Gordon was always researching and found that six rounds of chemo alone were just as effective and didn't carry radiation's risk of secondary cancers. In addition, Kirsten raved about Dr. Gordon's nurse, Michelle Balla. Kirsten saw her nurse more than anyone else at the hospital, so she advised us to find a good physician but especially a good nurse. Over the next six months, I found her advice to ring very true. I spent most of my time at the hospital with my nurse, so finding a great one was crucial.

Even though we heard Hodgkin's treatment was pretty standard no matter which doctor we chose, my dad wanted me to use the best oncologist and hospital we could find. Though doctors near campus could have treated me, my dad felt good about what Kirsten said and wanted to see if we could use Dr. Gordon. In addition, my older sister Katie was completing a child life specialist internship in Atlanta, and she told us that radiation often leads to other kinds of cancer later in life. My grandma had breast cancer in her fifties, so my gene pool already sucked, and my family figured if I had to undergo treatment for my current cancer, there was no reason to increase my odds for a secondary cancer down the road. We liked the idea that Dr. Gordon only used chemotherapy.

We called Kirsten back and asked if we could have Dr. Gordon's phone number. Her mom did us one better, saying she would call the next day to see if he would see us. We struggled to wrap our minds around everything that was happening and all the steps we had to take, but we knew finding a good doctor was the first step and that he would help us with the details from there. Since it was the day before Thanksgiving and a holiday weekend, Ms. Friedl said she'd leave a message, but then we would have to wait for a few days. I would fly back to school on Sunday night, so we had really hoped we'd be able to formulate a game plan while together, but since that couldn't happen, we waited.

A STRANGE THANKSGIVING

Those next few days were like an out-of-body experience for me. Upon hearing my diagnosis, I remember feeling too young for something like cancer. I mean, *Doesn't cancer happen to little kids who get leukemia, middle-aged women who get breast cancer, or old people who are in failing health anyway?* I naively wondered.

On Thanksgiving, my extended family gathered for dinner at our house, and we all hung out in the kitchen talking and hugging for a long time before sitting down to eat. My cousins and I bet how many times my grandma would cry, and given that she cried while watching *Pinocchio*, I bet we'd see tears at least five times. As she entered, my grandma immediately welled up. Since she was genuinely upset for me, my cousins and I tried our best to conceal our smiles as we noted that one cry was officially on the books. That definitely helped lighten the mood. Soon, everyone gathered around and prayed for me, my family, and our feast.

Over the rest of Thanksgiving break, my family and I hung out, talking through our options and how things might play out. My parents told me they wanted me to stay at school if that's what I really wanted. I'm so grateful they could see beyond their own desires to know that finishing college would be best for me, though being so far away during treatment would be extremely taxing on them. My parents knew that with their full-time jobs and most of my friends away at school, if I stayed home to undergo treatment in Dallas, I would probably be bored and depressed. They thought it best for me to finish college, stay surrounded by my friends and great community at Wheaton, and complete my treatment in Chicago. We didn't quite know how scheduling would work, how many tests I'd need before starting treatment, or even which doctor I would see yet, but my parents said if I stayed at Wheaton, they would come up for treatments and be there whenever I needed.

As the break ended, my dad pledged to call Dr. Gordon on Monday until he got through, assuring me that we would figure things out. On Sunday, all five of us got in the car, and my dad drove us to the Dallas/Fort Worth airport. I fly a good amount, and though normally my parents drop me off at curbside check-in and pray for me before I go through security, that day my dad parked the car and we all went inside the airport together. We gathered right outside of the security line for the prayer-before-flight.

As we huddled up, my dad began to pray, and I think for the first time in my life I saw him cry. I mean, I'd seen him sort of get teary eyed in church during moving testimonies, but I had never seen him outright cry, much less in the middle of the airport. I was so touched by my parents' love. My mom had to pick up where my dad left off because he couldn't recover his voice through his sobs. What a picture of God's love for us and the pain He feels when His children suffer trials. At that moment, I understood that my mom and dad would have traded places with me in an instant, and yet, they couldn't. I think the Lord feels the same way for us, too. After all, He sent His only Son to die in our place because He loved us that much. Just as my parents were so torn apart by seeing me suffer, so, too, the Lord hurts with us.

My mom finished the prayer, and we stood by security hugging for a while. It took great strength for my family to watch me walk away through security, heading back to Chicago when we'd just found out I had cancer. Though I'd flown back and forth from Dallas to Chicago countless times over the previous three years and I technically went back as a normal college student after a holiday, there was something profoundly different about *this* trip. At this point, I wasn't sure if I'd be finished flying to Chicago for a while—or forever, depending on how treatment went. The holiday and family times were over, school would resume the next day, and suddenly I was hit with a daunting reality: I was flying back into one of the most surreal and life-altering situations imaginable.

In The Word:

- **Psalm 27:3, 13-14** "Though an army besiege me, my heart will not fear; though war break out against me, even then will I be confident…. I am still confident of this: I will see the goodness of the Lord in the land of the living. Wait for the Lord; be strong and take heart and wait for the Lord."
- **Psalm 46:1-3** "God is our refuge and strength, an ever-present help in trouble. Therefore, we will not fear, though the earth give way and the mountains fall into the heart of the sea, though its waters roar and foam and the mountains quake with their surging."
- **Hebrews 13:8** "Jesus Christ is the same yesterday and today and forever."

On the Web:

- The National Cancer Institute (www.cancer.gov) has glossaries of cancer terms, extremely helpful planning books about treatment, and other useful tips.
- The American Cancer Society (www.cancer.org) is a national organization with branches in most major cities and in many suburbs. They sponsor a new site where you can input your diagnosis information and connect with others facing your same situation.
- The Planet Cancer (www.planetcancer.com) offers resources for young adults from message boards and latest news to "Top 10 Lists" (i.e. "Top 10 List: You've Joined a Cheap HMO;" "Top 10 Worst Responses to Hearing Someone has Cancer"), and other humorous tips.
- The i'm too young for this! Foundation (www.stupidcancer. org) hosts an annual cancer summit, forums on cancer, and the "Stupid Cancer Show," as well as selling merchandise such as wristbands, t-shirts, and of course, The Cancer Card.

CHAPTER 2

The "C" Word

Monday, December 1, 2008

"My comfort in my suffering is this: Your promise preserves my life" (Psalm 119:50).

Well, my return to Wheaton quickly reminded me that I no longer remained in the comforts of home as everywhere around me was—and still is—covered in white. *Welcome back; hope you like the snow.* This post will be short, as I'm dealing with the consequences of taking my Thanksgiving break very literally, but I have some great news to report.

This morning, after what would have been a movie-worthy succession of phone calls and messages between my dad, Dr. Santi, two hospitals, and me (all within the span of about forty-five minutes), we finally scheduled an appointment with the oncologist. On Wednesday at 3 p.m. my parents and I will see Dr. Leo Gordon, the doctor Kirsten Friedl used who has done tons of research while specializing in Hodgkin's disease. Here's a fun fact for you: he works out of Northwestern Memorial Hospital in downtown Chicago, the same hospital featured in the movie *While You Were Sleeping.* My family and I were randomly watching it last week over break when I shouted, "Wait! Go back! Look at the name on the hospital door!" Clearly etched on the glass was "Northwestern Memorial Hospital," and we decided that was an omen. With this appointment, we should know more about when treatment will start, what it will look like, and what else to expect. I want to thank you again for all of your prayers! The hospital said Dr. Gordon is heavily booked but likes to see patients if they're within a week of the biopsy and results, so he wants to see me. That's a huge praise!

Your prayers really have been so huge, so I ask for prayer Wednesday that the appointment will go well, we'll figure out all the details, and my parents will travel safely from Dallas and back after the appointment (It's supposed to be a snowy day and one of my parents—who will remain nameless—hates to fly). Thanks for moving me to tears again and again and for partnering with me and my family in this! God is doing a great work, and as my friend Caitlin said, "In a year or two we're just gonna be like, 'What? Cancer? Oh yeah, I forgot that happened.'"

On Christ the solid Rock I stand,

Hannah
Posted at 5:17 p.m.

BACK TO REAL LIFE

Walking across Wheaton's frozen campus on Monday after Thanksgiving break, I juggled calls from Dr. Santi, my dad, the hospital in Wheaton where I had my biopsy, and Northwestern Memorial Hospital trying to figure out which doctor I'd see, when I'd see him or her, and where said doctor would be. I reached chapel, relieved to turn my phone on silent and forget about so many details for a moment. When chapel ended, I checked my phone and saw that I'd missed two calls from my dad. I headed back to my house, and by the time I called him back, he had a plan. In two days, my parents would fly to Chicago for my first appointment with Dr. Gordon downtown at Northwestern. Though I dreaded starting treatment since I knew it wouldn't be fun, I was relieved to finally have some answers and a clearer picture of the future.

On Wednesday, I went to my Drugs and Society class, had breakfast with friends, attended chapel, then went to my Senior Seminar literature course. Though later that afternoon I would meet my oncologist to discuss the fact that I had cancer, life went on and I had to keep up with it. I couldn't meet my parents at the airport, but fortunately, my mom's best friend and her husband, Sandy and Al Boulden, were in town at their Chicago condo, so they picked up my parents. After class, I drove out to the Bouldens' place, said quick hellos and goodbyes, ushered my parents into my Chevy Tahoe, and made my way downtown.

First, I headed to the hotel where my parents would stay for the night before catching an early flight home for work the next morning. They stayed at the same hotel we'd used for my college visits and each subsequent trip my parents made to come see me. It was like our familiar haven amidst the big city bustle. After checking in and dropping off their bags, my dad asked where the hospital was, and I replied that I wasn't *exactly* sure but it was definitely downtown *somewhere*. I got out my phone and mapped out the hospital's location while we took the elevator to the lobby.

As we walked outside to hail a taxi, my phone pinpointed the hospital's location. I stopped, remarking that a cab was probably unnecessary. To our surprise, the hospital stood a block and a half north on the same street as our hotel, and as my parents looked at the map to verify my information, I looked north and pointed. Northwestern was a two minute walk away with traffic lights, and though I had stayed at this hotel numerous times over the past three years of college, somehow I had never noticed that it nearly stood on the hospital's campus. In fact, we later found out the hotel had a "Northwestern Hospital Rate" for patients which we would make use of for my subsequent appointments.

We walked the block and a half to the hospital and asked for directions to the Robert H. Lurie Cancer Center once inside, discovering it was on the twenty-first floor at the top of the building. Since we hadn't figured our commute to the hospital would only take two minutes, we arrived at the waiting area with ample time to spare. We checked in, received a pager, made ourselves comfortable, and checked out the place. Comfy chairs and couches in rustic fall hues filled the large waiting room, and various people were seated, all waiting. Some sat in wheelchairs, a couple used oxygen tanks, and others stood out as cancer patients because they wore scarves or hats on their shorn scalps. The reality that cancer sucks started to set in as I saw so many others in a similar—or far worse—boat as me. Not wanting to think about what awaited me, I walked past the front desk to a row of windows overlooking downtown and Lake Michigan. As I peered out, I was struck by how glad I was to be in Chicago having this consultation rather than at home.

After a while, I went back to sit with my parents, and I tried to take it all in: I was waiting to meet with an oncologist *because I had cancer*. I struggled to fully embrace that reality; after all, I met with Dr. Gordon exactly one week after finding out I had cancer, and the days between were filled to the brim with Thanksgiving festivities, traveling back to school, resuming classes, and trying to sort through hundreds of details. That didn't leave much time for the gravity of my situation to sink in.

I looked down at my pager—the same kind restaurants hand out while customers wait for a table—but rather than hungrily awaiting the moment when it would go off and I could eat, this time I silently willed the pager to keep its loud mouth shut, or else. I guess my mind control abilities need honing, because my pager buzzed right then, and a nurse led my parents and me through a door, down a long hallway, and into a consultation room. We waited, trying to picture what Dr. Gordon would look like, what he'd say, and what would happen next. My dad went over the questions we needed to ask, and soon Dr. Gordon entered.

MEETING THE ONCOLOGIST

My dad is an attorney who specializes in details, so he had the foresight to make a list of questions for Dr. Gordon. My dad knew I don't so much focus on the details, so I'm glad he took the initiative in covering all the bases for me. On our list were questions about my outlook, treatment options, scheduling, and our concerns. We figured, when faced with cancer, there are no stupid questions. After all, it's *cancer*; it's not like I had the common cold.

Our meeting with Dr. Gordon went smoothly, considering the circumstances. Dr. Gordon spent a full hour with us. He talked through the background of my disease, explained the planned treatment regimen, and answered every single question we threw at him—and we had many. Dr. Gordon explained that doctors aren't exactly sure what causes Hodgkin's disease. They know it has some sort of link to the Epstein Barr Virus which often causes mono, but the link between the virus and Hodgkin's is unclear because most people contract the virus in their lifetimes, but only about 40% of patients with Hodgkin's have had mono. In addition, sometimes doctors find the disease among siblings, but the percentage also isn't enough to be causal, though some link exists. Basically, he told us, doctors don't know what causes Hodgkin's and it's relatively rare compared to other types of cancer, but despite those two strikes against it, doctors usually know how to cure the disease. That's why, he explained, if you have to have cancer, you want Hodgkin's.

Unfortunately, that didn't mean it was like some types of skin cancer where I could just apply a daily cream and call it a day. I'd still have to undergo difficult treatment. My nurse Michelle Balla came into the room after Dr. Gordon left to describe what that entailed, and she stayed and talked to us for forty more minutes. Right away, I noticed her button proclaiming "Cancer sucks," concluding, *I think I'm gonna like her.* Michelle explained that she would administer my chemo and that each treatment would take a few hours. My specific treatment was called ABVD, an acronym for four different drugs administered through an IV. The chemo would poison and eventually kill the cancerous cells in my lymph nodes. Each treatment would happen every two weeks, and two chemo treatments equaled one round, so one round a month. My treatment plan called for either four or six rounds depending on my prognosis. Following her explanation, Michelle asked if we had any more questions.

My main question was what, exactly, chemotherapy was. Though I knew people who had undergone chemo, I didn't really know what it entailed. I figured it involved rays—you know, like radiation is one kind, X-rays are another, MRIs and CTs are more?—until we learned in my Drugs and Society course that "chemotherapy" refers to any sort of drug treatment. When people use the term today, they usually refer to drug therapy for cancer patients, but I knew from class that chemo could take many forms: pills, intravenously (IV), given into the body cavity, or a shot.

Michelle explained that chemotherapy kills all fast-growing cells in a person's body. Unfortunately, the drugs can't differentiate between the good fast-growing cells and the cancerous ones, hence the many unfortunate side effects of chemo. Hair, finger and toe nails, mouth cells, stomach cells, and cancer cells are all fast-growing (hair grows much faster than, say, bones or organs). Chemotherapy targets all of those fast-growing cells, killing anything in its path and causing hair loss, brittle fingernails, mouth sores, nausea, and other side effects along the way.

Michelle answered our final questions, and we discussed whether I would receive a port or not. A port is a round disc placed on a patient's skin and surgically connected to a large vein through which a nurse can easily administer chemo. That sounded like a good idea, but I needed to start treatment the next week, and with exams and everything else I had going on, I didn't have time for surgery before my first treatment. Once chemo started its work, my immune system would be too low for surgery. So we closed the book on that option (though I would later regret the decision when my veins stopped cooperating and it took thirty minutes to even prep for treatment). I was happy to finally have a better picture of the next six months. Michelle has an infectious personality, and I was glad to have someone so personable and talkative to sit with me and nurse me through the many hours of chemo I faced. Right from the start, my parents and I felt great about the excellent knowledge, bedside manner, and expertise of Dr. Gordon and Michelle.

Dr. Gordon returned with some final information. He suspected we caught my lymphoma at an early stage before it spread to my abdomen or other organs, but we had to make sure by testing my bone marrow and blood first. We decided I would drive back to the hospital the following day to get my blood tested, have a bone marrow biopsy, and schedule a smattering of other tests necessary to stage my cancer before moving ahead with treatment.

Before leaving, I scheduled my first treatment for the following Thursday, December 11th. My main concern had been finishing college on time, and when we went ahead with treatment in Chicago, we also worried about what would happen if I had to finish treatment during the summer after the lease term on my house ended. With twelve chemo treatments to complete and one every two weeks, my final treatment was scheduled for Thursday, May 14th, four days after graduation. My family and I were amazed at God's great timing. If everything went according to plan, I would be able to graduate, finish chemo four days later, and move home without missing a beat.

My parents and I left Northwestern and headed back to their hotel room to rehash all the details again. Shortly thereafter, I had to return to Wheaton and study since I had exams in a week and a half. We prayed, hugged, and said goodbye, and I drove back to the suburbs feeling overwhelmed.

DECISIONS, DECISIONS...

When it comes to choosing a doctor, the task can be overwhelming. Many people find themselves at a loss because they haven't had a reason to see an oncologist before. Because I was away from home and hadn't seen a doctor in the Chicago area before, I relied on my connections. I found Dr. Santi through the Armstrongs' doctor, and I found Dr. Gordon through Kirsten, and I'm so grateful for them. I found out later that a couple of organizations help patients find doctors in their areas, some health insurance companies have referral services, and the Mayo

Clinic and the American Medical Association both have online resources for finding doctors, but I didn't know about them when I scrambled to find an oncologist. Thankfully, God provided.

A brochure I found early on encouraged patients to make their own decisions to avoid feeling helpless by letting others (or cancer) dictate their lives. I appreciated the advice and took it to heart. Now, it would have been ludicrous to think I knew more than my doctors when they spent decades studying, training for, and practicing medicine. Arguing with their every word wasn't my game plan. But when I could make my own choices, I did, whether about my activity level, what to eat, or which doctor I would see. I realized I wasn't in control of my future—God was, and the doctors had a lot of impact in that process, too—but I tried to maintain some say in my life when possible. I trusted in God's plan, and I trusted that my doctors knew what they were talking about. But, though doctors knew cancer and medicine better, I knew myself better. Staying engaged and making decisions helped me maintain a semblance of control rather than succumbing to passive surrender.

I know without a doubt Dr. Santi tried to look out for me by advising me to stay home for treatment because I'd have my family nearby. However, I know myself fairly well, so I know I did the right thing by staying in Chicago to complete chemotherapy. Was it difficult? Absolutely. Have I ever regretted it? No, not even once.

My mom and dad both worked full time, and my little sister attended high school. If I had stayed home for treatment, my parents would have taken off work to care for me as needed, but it's not like they could've called in sick for all of the long days when I felt terrible. On better days, since all of my friends from high school were away at college, I wouldn't have had anyone to hang out with. I would have sat at home bored, lonely, and miserable thinking about all my friends at Wheaton finishing school together and on the road to graduation. In short, I would have been depressed, and since attitude can significantly impact bodily health during cancer, being depressed would have been highly detrimental to my already deteriorating condition. After my first meeting with Dr. Gordon, I knew I was at the right hospital, seeing the right doctor, and surrounded by the best distractions and support up in Illinois, and that knowledge made a grueling journey much easier.

STAGING MY CANCER

Before I get too far ahead of myself, let me pause to highlight the barrage of tests I underwent before I could even start treatment. The tests would help determine my lymphoma's stage: stage I meant tumors in only one site, stage II meant tumors in multiple sites but all in the same half of my upper or lower diaphragm, stage III meant tumors in multiple sites across both halves of my diaphragm, and stage IV meant cancer in multiple sites and even permeating my bone marrow and organs. From my initial CT scan and X-ray, Dr. Gordon saw a couple of tumors under my sternum and the two I first noticed above the left side of my collarbone, so he was pretty sure I had stage II Hodgkin's lymphoma. He didn't think the disease had spread further, but no one guesses with things like cancer, so he scheduled my bone marrow biopsy for the day after we first met.

Of all the tests I endured, the bone marrow biopsy was my personal favorite (sarcasm heavily intended). On Thursday after class ended, my freshman teammate Kelly and I drove downtown to the hospital for the exam. Only as I made the final exit off the highway did I find out she had skipped class to accompany me. After I chided her for her actions with exams quickly approaching, Kelly reassured me she needed to be there with me and that her parents had even told her to skip class. I shook my head, amazed at all the trouble people were going to for me.

We arrived at the hospital and I met my nurse practitioner Sarah Miyata for the first time. She told me she'd be overseeing my biopsy and that it wouldn't be too bad. Surprised, I asked her if she'd had cancer—after all, typically people only have biopsies when there's a cancer threat. Sarah said she hadn't but underwent a bone marrow biopsy to know what it felt like. I took her word, but hearing her say she had one done simply to know what it felt like should have clued me in to the fact that she was hardcore and probably not to be trusted in matters of pain. Red flag number one. She told me that she and her assistant would take a fragment of my pelvic bone from my back to test the marrow within for cancer.

I found out her assistant had graduated from Texas A&M University, so we quickly bonded, but when I asked what brought her to Chicago (assuming something normal like graduate school or her residency), she told me she wanted to experience the seasons of Chicago. That should have been my second red flag that something was not right. Who voluntarily chooses to live where -20 degree weather and snowstorms are annual occurrences? That morning alone it was 14 degrees outside and winter had just begun, so if this woman moved here because she *wanted* that, then both members of my biopsy team had issues.

Sarah started by numbing a spot on the left side of my lower back. "It'll just feel like a bee sting," she explained. Apparently we both forgot that bee stings hurt like crazy, and she forgot to mention that said "bee sting" would travel up the length of my back as the shot numbed the entire left side of my back. It actually felt like a *swarm* of bees stinging me, and the procedure hadn't even started.

Later, when I called my parents, I blurted out, "I got cored!" They were understandably confused, so I went on to explain my bone marrow biopsy. It's basically like coring an apple, only instead of taking out the core of a piece of fruit, doctors core out a piece of bone from a person's back. Despite the fact that they had numbed my back and the nerves around my bone, I could still feel the pressure of them pushing on my back and, for lack of better words, corkscrewing into my bone to extract a fragment from my hip. The whole time I lay on my stomach, I felt like saying, *Um, I kind of wanted to* keep *all of my bones, thank you very much*, but I didn't think that would be appropriate nor appreciated.

The procedure wasn't the most painful thing I've ever gone through— that honor goes to a post-chemo shot I had to give myself—but it was definitely the most disturbing. Sarah and her assistant probably should have gone ahead and put me under anesthesia so that I wasn't conscious of what they were doing the whole time. It must be pretty disgusting to everyone involved, too, because at one point, Sarah asked, "Are you okay?" to which I responded meekly in the affirmative. However, she politely informed me that she was talking to my teammate Kelly sitting a few feet away.

I thought, *How about you ask* me *since you're digging a hole in my bone?!* but as if she could read my mind, Sarah explained that the biggest issues with bone marrow biopsies occur with friends and family members in the room. Apparently the procedure is more disgusting to view than to undergo because Sarah had seen many friends and family members pass out or throw up after watching. Kelly deserves a medal for being unfazed—or at least for putting on a great poker face—as she asked me all kinds of questions and brought up various discussion points when I begged her to distract me.

When the bone fragment was extracted and I could turn over onto my back, Sarah asked if I wanted to see what it looked like. I wasn't going to let her core me for nothing, so I said yes. My bone looked like a toothpick in a jar, and I skeptically wondered what now filled in the gap the bone fragment left. Initially Sarah had planned on taking bone from both sides of my back, but she said she got a great fragment, and since that one sliver looked free from lymphoma, she'd only do the one side. Had she biopsied my right side as well, I think I would have passed out or hurt someone once I knew what to expect. Though happy the lymphoma hadn't spread to my bone marrow, I was more relieved that the procedure ended and I could get the heck out of there before someone else tried to do something barbaric to me.

MORE TESTS

Before I left, I scheduled one test for the following day—yes, that would mean spending three days in a row downtown at Northwestern—and four more tests for the following Tuesday. Though I knew cancer was an involved process, I hadn't imagined so many tests required to simply start treatment. By the time treatment actually rolled around, I was running on autopilot.

The next day began with a multi gated acquisition scan, or MUGA scan, which helps determine the heart's health and functionality before bombarding it with harmful chemotherapy. The MUGA scan felt much like CT scans and MRIs. Technicians hooked me up to an IV and ran fluid which included a radioactive marker that entered my bloodstream, showing my heart's circulation and efficiency while I passed through a scanner.

The next Tuesday, after my classes ended I returned once more to the hospital for a marathon day of testing. Here's how it broke down: I began with an X-ray on the fourth floor of the hospital from 1:30 to 2:30 p.m.; I had a PET scan from 2:45 to 4:45 p.m. on the eighth floor; I had to go back to the sign-in desk on that *same* floor to check in for my pulmonary function test at 4:45 p.m.; and I finished the night back on the fourth floor for a CT scan from 5:30 to 7:30 p.m.

My first test, the chest X-ray, felt like no big deal after all of the other tests I underwent. X-rays are fast, painless since they don't involve needles, and pretty easy. I wondered what the point of the test was because I'd only heard of X-rays for issues like bone breaks and fractures, but I found out chest X-rays can also show glimpses of the heart and lungs, helping identify cancer there.

The positron emission tomography, or PET scan, reigns as my favorite because, though technicians hooked me up to an IV and my veins were tired of all the poking and prodding, the test was pretty relaxing. Technicians inject patients with radioactive glucose and then use imaging to see where that sugar travels. Tumors metabolize sugar very quickly, so PET scans highlight the radioactive sugar in tumors as bright colors on a computer screen. Physical activity can give a false positive for tumors since it shows up on the scan, so patients have to be very still for an hour as the sugar works its magic. The nurse banned me from walking around, talking on the phone, writing, or generally moving too much because those actions could throw off the results. She even stopped me from writing a paper for class because my arm might move too much. Instead, I literally had to lie back in a chair and rest. *Forced relaxation? Um, yes, please! Sign me up for more of those.*

In the pulmonary function test, I had to breathe into a tube so a technician could assess my lung capacity. One of the drugs in my chemo regimen had the potential to damage and scar my lungs, so the doctors needed an initial benchmark to know how my lungs were holding up later during treatment. The test included various exercises—from holding my breath then bursting out to panting like a dog—as I sat in something I can only describe as a human-sized egg chamber. All of the fun in the PF test came from the woman instructing me on the tasks I had to perform. I'm pretty sure she should host educational TV or something based on her vivid explanations and animated examples of what I needed to do.

Exhausted from the day of tests, I headed downstairs for my final scan of the night, the CT. This scan helped my doctor assess whether the lymphoma had spread to my abdomen, spleen, or other organs in the lower half of my body. I asked the technician how this test differed from all the previous ones, and he tried to explain it to me in normal, human language. He said a CT is like slicing up a loaf of bread, cutting off the end piece, and looking down the shaft of the loaf, piece by piece...only in scan form and without any actual slicing. So basically, a CT scan creates a layered image of a person's organs in great detail. That may not be the most technical or scientific way to explain the scan, but it helped me visualize the scenario and made me feel better about undergoing five different types of procedures.

At the end of my marathon day of tests, I felt most proud that I chugged the two bottles of barium sulfate needed to highlight contrast in my CT scan like a champ, especially given that I'm a super picky eater. I downed both bottles of the liquid (supposedly masked by a "berry flavor") without

once gagging or thinking about throwing up. Luckily I didn't realize at
the time how many more bottles of the chalky chemical substance I'd
imbibe over the next few years.

All of these tests needed to take place before I could start my first chemo
two days later. It was a blessing to move ahead so quickly and complete
all of these tests within a few days, but I went home in a less-than-ideal
mood. I headed to my room and crashed, thoroughly beat. Fortunately,
I didn't have time to worry about my impending chemo because I was
exhausted, and somewhere between all of the staging tests, my upcoming
treatment, and needing sleep, I still had to finish the last three days of my
fall semester classes before exams the following week.

CANCER, REALLY?

The next day I walked into chapel and spotted my teammate Ashlie
on the way to our assigned seats. She volunteered to use her last of
nine chapel skips to sit with me instead of in her own seat. After a
moment of hesitation, I took her up on the offer, and I'm glad I did.
Before our chaplain started praying, he announced, "We just found
out last week that senior Hannah McGinnis, who many of you might
know as the co-captain of the volleyball team, was diagnosed with
Hodgkin's lymphoma...." He said more, but I stopped listening because
the announcement caught me off guard. I knew the chaplains would pray
for me in chapel, and most friends already knew about the diagnosis, so
neither of those things surprised me, but actually hearing those words
out loud felt surreal, like an out-of-body experience.

I mean, I'd known I had cancer for a couple of weeks, but something
about hearing our chaplain voice that reality made me think, *That's
not some random girl I've never met; that's* me *he's talking about.* Over
the past three years at Wheaton, the chaplains prayed for countless
students, but I never imagined I'd be added to that list someday. When
the chaplain announced my name, Ashlie reached over and grabbed my

hand, squeezing it and wrapping her other arm around my shoulder as my eyes filled with tears. Though I'd been busy with tests and doctors for over a month, hearing the reality of what was happening in my life, while sitting in chapel as I'd so regularly done for three years, made the gravity of my situation hit home. I'm incredibly grateful for Ashlie and for the perfect timing that on this particular day we ran into each other and she took an absence from her assigned seat to be with me.

My whole experience with cancer felt like that: very surreal. The whole time, I felt as if I inhabited someone else's life or was the protagonist in some dramatic Christian fiction novel. Like many other trials in life, cancer happens to *other* people, not us—or so we assume.

One night the week after Christmas, my sisters, my mom, and I all sat around watching TV in our family room. My dad walked in after work and started washing his hands in the adjacent kitchen. He looked over at us and said, "Hannah, what in the *world* are you doing with cancer?"

I paused the TV show as we all turned toward my dad with quizzical looks on our faces. I said, "Um...good question?" and everyone laughed. My dad explained that, while sitting at his desk that morning, the crazy reality of my cancer struck him. When he sat back and thought about it, he wondered what in the world I was doing with cancer. Though the first appointment to the first treatment spanned a month's time, cancer still snuck up on us, catching us off guard and leaving us to wonder how that happened. His question was big, but valid. How on *earth* did I—did you, did anyone—get cancer?

Singer Ben Rector captures how I felt upon receiving my diagnosis. In "When a Heart Breaks," he sings, "I heard the doctor, but what did he say? I knew I was fine about this time yesterday." I love those simple lines because they describe the craziness of dealing with something like cancer: *Yes, I heard the doctor correctly, but* what *did he say? This time yesterday I was fine and now...cancer?* It's not an issue of mishearing or misunderstanding; it's incomprehension of a whole other sort, one of unfathomable disbelief.

During the many waiting periods I've spent in my oncologist's office, I've seen all kinds of fliers and pamphlets on various topics about cancer. Two that caught my eye on a recent visit were titled "How Does Cancer Affect My Ability to Have Children?" and "Starting a Family After Cancer." *Seriously, I have to worry about stuff like that now?* At the age of twenty-one, these are probably the last questions I ever would have thought about prior to cancer. Even now, I have a tendency to think this kind of stuff happens to anyone but me. However, clearly that's not the case. Having gone through cancer, I now try to expect the unexpected. Apparently nothing's too far-fetched anymore; just about anything can happen to anyone.

While studying my Bible, Psalm 9:20 caught my attention one day: "Strike them with terror, O Lord; let the nations know they are but men." How does that possibly relate to cancer? Well, contextually, it doesn't. David prays for God to take revenge on his enemies, and while cancer might be the enemy, I'm not saying we should pray for God to strike cancer with terror. I mean, it could be fun, but that's not the point. The second half of the verse gets to the point. David prays God would show the nations that they are "but men:" mortal, frail, and prone to breaking so they will see in contrast how great God is. I paused my reading and asked myself, *Do I know this? Do I know that I am but man?*

I think the first time I confronted my sheer frailty was when I faced cancer. Other people see their impermanence early on in life through car accidents, deaths in the family, and other trials. I had seen my fragility through injuries and other trials before, but for the first time, cancer brought me face to face with the fact that I could die at any moment.

Though my type and stage of lymphoma gave me a good outlook, without treatment, Hodgkin's would kill me. This verse made me realize not just how fragile life is—I'd had some friends, relatives, and campers pass away and show me that—but what I saw clearly for the first time was just how fragile my *own* life really is. We try to avoid the thought that we are but men. While that reality is scary, I think it's beneficial because it keeps us relying on the Lord to physically protect our lives. Even now, it's amazing to me that, having survived cancer, sometimes I forget how fragile my life is when I should know that every day—every second, really—is a gift.

WORDS OF PEACE

I fell into bed Wednesday night both physically and emotionally exhausted. Suddenly I realized Thursday would mark the first step on my road to healing. For the previous month and a half, all tests had been for the purpose of diagnosing and staging my disease, so while they were necessary, they didn't cure me, and they were draining. I turned on my iPod and put one of my favorite playlists on shuffle. "Whisper to Me" by Warren Barfield started playing, and though I liked the song, I hadn't really thought much about it before. That night, however, the lyrics struck me as incredibly poignant:

> I lay down and I close my eyes, but I won't go to sleep tonight. There's too much on my mind. Holy God, You seem to be twice as far away from me than You have ever been before. Hold me safely in Your arms and clear my crowded mind and whisper words of peace in the dark. Whisper to me. I'm afraid but they don't know it. I feel so weak but I can't show it. So here I lay crying out with tears. Hold me gently in Your arms and calm my beating heart and whisper words of hope in the dark. Whisper to me.[2]

Tears came to my eyes as I realized how perfect and timely this song was when I had far too much on my mind to fall asleep. I had very few moments when the full weight of cancer actually set in, and this was one of them. Though I wasn't having a major crisis of faith, as I confronted the reality of my situation, I couldn't understand God's plan. I felt weak, afraid, far from my family, and, though surrounded by people, still blazing a somewhat solitary path through cancer. I needed God to clear my mind of so many overwhelming and heavy thoughts, whispering His peace to me and holding me in His arms. I left the song on repeat, and finally, I fell asleep, nervous but ready to get the next day over with.

In the Word:

- **Psalm 29:11** "The Lord gives strength to His people; the Lord blesses His people with peace."
- **Psalm 59:16** "But I will sing of Your strength, in the morning I will sing of Your love; for You are my fortress, my refuge in times of trouble."
- **Proverbs 14:30a** "A heart at peace gives life to the body."
- **Isaiah 41:10** "So do not fear, for I am with you; do not be dismayed, for I am your God. I will strengthen you and help you; I will uphold you with my righteous right hand."

On the Web:

- The American Medical Association's DoctorFinder program provides a list of doctors you can research (www.ama-assn.org and look for the DoctorFinder link).
- Check out websites on specific cancers for links to doctors and other information. For instance, the American Society of Hematology (ASH) has a link to "Find a Hematologist" on their website (www.hematology.org).
- Cancer*Care*, Inc. (www.cancercare.org) offers brief tips on everything from coping with side effects to financial planning for cancer.
- The Mayo Clinic (www.mayoclinic.com) is a comprehensive and well-respected organization for finding out more details on types of cancer, types of treatment related to different diagnoses, and other helpful advice from doctors.

CHAPTER 3

Let the Healing Begin

Friday, December 12, 2008

"O Israel, put your hope in the LORD, for with the LORD is unfailing love and with Him is full redemption" (Psalm 130:7).

One down, eleven to go. When you think of it like that, it's manageable, right? Plus, "12" was always my volleyball number. I don't know if I'd call it lucky, but it is a very recurring number in my life, and as hokey as this sounds, it's endearing. So, of course there *would* be twelve chemos to go through.

I'd love prayer for no nausea tomorrow and to figure out the details of my treatment in Dallas. Two weeks from yesterday is Christmas Day, so I need treatment the day before or after Christmas, and I'd rather do it on the 26th so that I feel okay on Christmas. I'd love continued prayers for my parents, Kevin and Brenda, and my two sisters, Madelyn and Katie. Also, while you're at it, my extended family could probably use prayer, too, since we're all really close, and I know this is hard on them, too.

In about a week, my blood counts (both white and red) will drop due to the fact that I've been poisoned (in a good way... that sounds so wrong), so I'll be susceptible to infections. Dr. Gordon wants patients to keep living life, so I won't have to skip every chapel nor avoid every crowd of over ten people or anything. In fact, most of the infections I could get would come from my own system, since with blood counts down, my body isn't fighting off the 80% of infections it does every day that I never know about. I mean, I'm not gonna say, "Go ahead, please use my sleeve for your runny nose," or anything, but I don't have to be a germaphobe. So, another long-term prayer request is that I wouldn't get sick throughout this whole process. Once my counts go down next week, they will stay down. They'll rise again a little (thus the two week intervals between treatments), and it's safe to continue treating with low counts. Still, a minor sickness to anyone else could mean a stay in the hospital for me. There are so many aspects of healing to pray for—the end result being remission, free from my not-so-friendly resident Hodgkin's disease—but also prayer for limited, or even nonexistent side effects, and that I won't get *other* infections along the way, too. Complicated, I know.

Beyond my physical health, I'd love continued prayer for perseverance and especially to know my limits. One of my greatest weaknesses is overcommitting, which doesn't sound so bad, but it is when I spread myself too thin and then shortchange each area in which I'm involved. I can't say no— not because I'm so good at heart and really selfless—no, no, only because I am pretty much Katherine Heigl's character Jane in the movie *27 Dresses*. She doesn't have the courage to say no but then admonishes herself afterward for saying yes. Anyway, cancer *is* going to slow me down, and when it does, I'd love prayer to rest in where God has me, to know my limits, and to accept them with grace. Finally, please pray for me to lean on God and bring Him glory with all of the opportunities to share His faithfulness, that I would take hold of those opportunities instead of taking them for myself and my own gratification.

Love you, thank you, and miss you. Thanks for your faithfulness to me and my family, and have a blessed weekend! (And you can take a breath now; I am finished.)

On Christ the solid Rock I stand,

Hannah
Posted at 7:31 p.m.

THE REAPING

When I woke up on Thursday morning, chemo day had arrived and the reaping was upon me. I went to my morning class, emailed my Corinthians professor my final research paper at 11:30 a.m., stopped back by my house to change into comfy clothes and grab a care package my aunts had sent, and then drove to the airport to pick up my mom. She got in the car and we headed to the hospital, making it just in time for my 1:30 p.m. appointment. The day was a blur, but that worked out well because with so much going on, I didn't have time to worry about the fact that I had chemotherapy later.

I guess reality *actually* set in when I stepped into the elevator to the Robert H. Lurie Cancer Center for my first chemotherapy treatment. I turned to my mom and said, "Wow, this is it...it all begins today." Everything felt surreal, but what was most bizarre was how routine the process seemed in the end. No fanfare met me at the elevator door, and all of heaven and earth didn't stop moving because I faced chemo. Instead, I moved fluidly forward through each step of treatment, as if being willed on by some invisible force.

Rick and Lynda Armstrong, my teammate Ruth's parents, had been my "Wheaton family" over the previous three years. They'd taken me on vacation with their family, cheered me on in volleyball, offered me encouragement and advice, and served as my landlords during my senior year. When I told them about my diagnosis, they responded by telling my parents that they were committed to attending every treatment they could with me. My parents would fly in for at least every other treatment, and the Armstrongs would attend those also if my parents wanted. They assured us they would fill in for my parents by taking off work, driving me downtown to the hospital, sitting with me through chemo, and taking me back to Wheaton afterward.

They were amazing. There's no way I can repay them for taking care of me as if I was their own child, and there's no way my parents can ever repay them for the peace of mind they provided. The Armstrongs knew it would be helpful for me to have a consistent presence at appointments. In case issues arose later, if I felt out of it and couldn't recall what my medical team said, or if all the details became too overwhelming, the Armstrongs could help me fill in the gaps and sort through information. Mr. Armstrong decided to attend my first treatment, so he called to let us know he was upstairs on the cancer floor as we walked into the hospital.

Shortly after my mom and I arrived, met Mr. Armstrong, and checked in, my pager buzzed and a nurse took me back to a lab to get my blood drawn. Doctors first have to ensure that a patient's body can take the poison they're about to administer, of course. After blood work, I rejoined my mom and Mr. Armstrong in the waiting area, and fifteen minutes later my pager buzzed again, this time signaling that chemo time had arrived. We headed back to a room with a bed, an IV pole, a TV, and two chairs for guests. I glanced around, noticing how sterile everything smelled and looked.

Michelle came in and hooked me up to two IV bags: one full of saline to help hydrate my system and dilute the chemo, and the other an anti-nausea drug. She found a vein in my forearm and let the saline and anti-nausea fluids run. After a few seconds, I tasted the saline in my mouth, and though others describe it as metallic, I felt like I was drinking my contact solution. While the saline wasn't a problem then, it became one of my least favorite things about treatment, and I learned to bring peppermints with me to mask the taste. I would pop one in and chew vigorously before and after she inserted the IV so I wouldn't taste it. To this day when I open up a pill bottle emitting that smell and reminding me of that saline, nausea sweeps over me as I remember everything associated with that odor and taste.

After the saline and anti-nausea drugs had run for a while, Michelle came over with a tray holding three syringes and one additional IV bag. One of the syringes was red, one was clear, and another had a faint yellow hue.

Those, I would learn, were the Adriamycin, bleomycin, and vinblastine drugs in my ABVD regimen, while the IV bag was the dacarbazine. Michelle connected the first syringe to my IV and slowly administered the drug until the syringe emptied, checking to make sure I didn't feel any pain. If chemo leaks outside of veins or is administered too quickly, it can damage veins, skin, and other parts of the arm that have a natural inclination to avoid poisons.

Following the first drug, she pushed the bleomycin and then the vinblastine one at a time. Finally, Michelle hooked up the IV bag from her tray, running it simultaneously with the bag of saline. Dacarbazine, Michelle explained, had to be infused at a slower rate and heavily diluted with the ever-flowing saline. It dripped over the course of about an hour, giving me a long time to sit back and wait for the effects of chemo to hit. Over the next eleven treatments, I would use that time to answer questions regarding treatment, watch movies, and catch up with friends, but during this first treatment, my mom, Mr. Armstrong, and I didn't say much.

I looked up at the IV bag, struck by how similar it looked to the saline next to it. Their similarities ended at outward appearances though. One was essentially poison, and the other was glorified saltwater. I stared and thought, *Hmmmm...that's the poison, it's moving into my veins, and it's healing me.* That's *chemo.*

I learned that day how very normal chemo actually is. I realize I sound crazy. *Chemo? Normal? Get serious, Hannah.* But somehow it seemed routine because the day kept going as if it was any other day. It was only after the fact, when I thought about it, that I couldn't believe what had just happened. Though treatment took its toll over time, while Michelle administered my chemo, it seemed far less involved than some of the scans and biopsies I'd undergone in the past two weeks. People receive chemotherapy and radiation every day, and though cancer treatment has the connotation of being scary and forbidden, it very easily became a normal part of my life over the next six months.

It's hard to describe how I felt. I wasn't horrifically nauseous or in pain, but I was acutely aware of the presence of chemicals in my body. I usually don't feel the effects of medicines too much, and when I do, they usually make me feel better, not out of it. With chemo, I felt as if someone had injected me with a bunch of bad chemicals or something foreign...which they kind of had. I felt really full because of all the saline I'd received over the course of two and a half hours, so I had to make multiple trips to the bathroom, IV pole and all. My mom noticed that my complexion changed during chemo. It started out full of color (or as much as possible given the Chicago winter and my understandable anxiety). As Michelle pushed the different chemo drugs, my face looked flushed with the Adriamycin, then all the color drained with the bleomycin, and after the dacarbazine had dripped for an hour, I looked gray and ashen.

While receiving chemotherapy, I first noticed the drugs' effects when my eyes moved too slowly. Like actors' lips that become unsynchronized with their words, my vision seemed out of sync with my eye movements. When I moved my eyes to the right or left, it was like my brain took a second to signal my vision to catch up. My eyes' disorientation was my first clue that cancer treatment affects a whole lot more than just tumors.

When my IV bags emptied around 6 p.m., we said goodbye to Mr. Armstrong, left the hospital, and headed back to my house in Wheaton. We fought rush hour traffic out to the suburbs, but I was so out of it and exhausted that I slept through the gridlock. When we arrived back at my house, my mom made some chicken spaghetti, saving a pan for when I didn't feel well enough to cook in the coming weeks. After I ate dinner and drank lots of water, my mom and I retired to my room, and I fell asleep pretty easily as my mom settled into my futon. *One chemo down, eleven more to go*, I told myself before nodding off.

THE AFTERMATH

On Friday morning, the morning after my first rendezvous with chemo, I slept until 7:35 a.m.—much longer than planned—only leaving myself twenty-five minutes to get to my Drugs and Society class. On a normal college day, I would have had ten minutes to spare. I was one of those college kids who literally kept my jeans hanging over the back of my desk chair so I could grab them, find a t-shirt, and cover up with my North Face jacket all while running out the door. I've done my makeup the same way since high school, and I'm okay with my hair being a little unruly, so my morning routine was fast and easy. However, that first morning after chemo, I was smacked with the reality that cancer would unavoidably slow me down.

Chemo only stays in a person for forty-eight hours, so the first two days following treatment hold the greatest potential for nausea. I had to take three different anti-nausea drugs and two other medications to curb chemo's effects, and since taking them without food only added to my nausea, I slowly swallowed my medicine over the course of ten minutes while I ate. Afterwards I had to wait for the pills to kick in before I felt well enough to get up and move around. I learned to eat a granola bar, take my anti-nausea drugs, and then fall back asleep for thirty minutes to let the medicine kick in.

The best way I can describe how I felt the morning after chemo is this: think about when you have a stomach bug. The first day you might throw up and feel wretched, while the second day you're no longer throwing up but feeling generally sick, out of it, weak, and tired. I felt like I was in day two of a stomach bug. I didn't throw up nor writhe in pain, but I felt generally affected and as if I'd just been through some sort of illness.

I missed my two classes that morning and, per my mom's advice, slept until I felt better. Even at twenty-one, it's nice when your parents let you skip school. My mom only planned to stay through that night, but since I had a volleyball banquet the next day and wasn't doing as well as we had naively assumed, my mom wanted to stay with me. She said I had more on my plate than I could handle on a regular day *minus* chemo, so she couldn't leave me like this. She called American Airlines and asked to change her flight to Saturday or Sunday.

After about thirty seconds of giving her information to the agent on the phone, my mom lost it. Here's what I heard: "I have...I'm sorry... Okay, *(inhale)* I have a daughter...I'm so sorry *(fifteen second pause with intermittent sobs)*...my daughter just had her first chemo yesterday *(trail off into high-pitched squeal)*...." At that, the agent talked to a manager and waived any transfer fees or fare increases. God is so good...plus my mom's uncontrollable sobs and squeals probably helped. Later, we laughed at how that conversation didn't quite unfold as she envisioned, though it turned out surprisingly well.

My mom's kindergarteners and their parents had sent her with a large shopping bag full of goodies, and after she hung up with the airline agent, my mom collected herself as I sorted through the gifts. In the bag were kindergarten drawings, notes from students saying they loved and prayed for me, bookmarks, an angel topper for my Christmas tree, candy, and other gifts.

My mom found a tabletop book titled *What Cancer Cannot Do*. It was a collection of stories from different authors who talked about the many things cancer can't do. I liked the book because it reminded me that cancer could not steal my joy nor change how much the Lord loved and cared for me. As my mom flipped through it, she paused at one particular story and melted into tears once more. The author of this story was nervous about her first appointment with her oncologist, but her doctor—*Dr. Leo Gordon*—immediately put her at ease. No other story in the book listed specific details like hospital or doctors' names, but this one did, and my mom was overwhelmed. I saw that as yet another reason why it's a small world after all. But on this morning after my first treatment, following her phone meltdown and realization she would soon leave me, my mom felt as if God was comforting her, affirming that He had me right where I needed to be.

I nodded off again while my mom read through the rest of the stories, and when I woke up, I decided to test the waters. Since I hadn't been through chemo before, I wasn't sure what to expect. I decided if I started to sink, I could always head back to bed. So that afternoon I ran some errands with my mom because even though cancer had invaded my life, the world kept on going. I had my college volleyball banquet the next day, exams the next week, and a fifteen hour drive home for Christmas afterward, so I had miles to go before I slept. My mom drove me all over the suburbs of Chicago looking for a pair of heels to match my dress, presents for my volleyball coaches, and supplies for the banquet after-party at my house. She was an irreplaceable help, and there's no way I could have gone to my banquet or made it through exams without her aid.

THE BANQUET

On Saturday morning, I awoke, ate some apple sauce, and took my five medications again. Harrison, my banquet date, would be over at 10 a.m., so I needed to get moving because mornings after chemo played out in slo-mo. However, I quickly encountered the phenomena known as "chemo brain" that morning. My nurse Michelle always joked about having it when she forgot something or jumbled her words. Doctors and nurses have observed that, for some reason, many cancer patients feel more forgetful and have difficulty with cognitive function because of chemotherapy. My mom asked me about my plans for the day, and in my mind I knew what I wanted to say, but for some reason I couldn't communicate clearly. Frustrated, I mustered only a growl. My mom looked at me, unsure whether to laugh or be offended, and I immediately felt bad. She just wanted to help me, but I took out my frustration on her. I apologized and attempted to have more patience in the future when chemo brain set in—and it sure did. I have a razor sharp memory most of the time, so I hated being unable to recall a thought or voice what I wanted to say.

Thankfully, my mom understood my misdirected frustration and patiently waited for me to get ready. She fixed my hair like when I was in high school getting ready for a dance and helped me get dressed and with my makeup. When my teammate Kelli saw my hairdo, she said if all my hair fell out, this was a pretty great last hurrah at least. Harrison came over and we got in my Tahoe, picked up my teammates Brooke and Sarah and their dates, and headed downtown to Maggiano's for my final college volleyball banquet.

Miraculously, I survived it. While to others a volleyball banquet probably sounds a little frivolous in light of something like cancer, I needed to attend and wrap up my volleyball career. Plus, I didn't want cancer to dictate my entire life. I sat with my friends, ate great Italian food, and took a ton of pictures. I even gave a speech in which I tearfully thanked my teammates for their help and reflected that, despite such a turbulent season, my teammates were like family and I was honored to have led them.

Later, everyone headed back to my house and found a winter wonderland awaiting us, courtesy of my mom. She had hung Christmas lights all over the house, baked dozens of cookies, bought cookie decorations, found a bunch of chairs somewhere, cleaned my room, and made snacks for the fifteen volleyball players and our dates. We had a gingerbread house decorating contest and ate far too much sugar, capping off the night by watching a movie. I enjoyed the party but struggled to stay awake. When everyone left, though I tried to help clean up, no one would let me. I robotically walked back to my room and fell into bed, exhausted but grateful I had made it to my banquet and wrapped up twelve years of playing volleyball.

THE WALL

On Sunday morning, I didn't have the anti-nausea drugs to take anymore, so I just took my anti-heartburn and anti-constipation medicines, ate slowly, and tried to rally myself for the day. I didn't make it to church, and I knew my mom had to leave soon. Around lunchtime, her best friend Sandy showed up to take her to the Chicago O'Hare airport. As soon as she got in the car, my mom burst into tears knowing she was leaving me when I wasn't in great shape. She hated being unable to care for me. Sandy has one of the most compassionate hearts around, so then *she* lost it, and they cried together the entire half hour trip to O'Hare.

After they left I dressed for a tacky Christmas sweater party for K-Life, a high school ministry I volunteered with. At first I felt better than I had on the previous two days, but by the end of the event, I was miserable. I bowed out early, made it back to my house, and collapsed onto my futon. My activity on Friday and Saturday must have caught up with me because I was utterly beat. The first forty-eight hours post-chemo hadn't been *that* bad. I definitely felt weird and filled with chemicals, but I'd escaped the nausea and other horror stories people warned about on those couple of days. I'd made it out of the danger zone of the first forty-eight hours, so I figured it would only be smoother sailing with each passing day.

I was so wrong.

Instead, I spent the rest of Sunday, all of Monday, and Tuesday morning in bed feeling awful. I felt like I had the flu: my whole body ached, at one point I worried about blacking out, and I had the chills. I called my oncologist, and he said about 10-29% of Hodgkin's patients experience flu-like symptoms. *Great.* So I was one of only around seven thousand people annually to get this disease, and of them, I was in the additional minority of having to feel flu-like. My luck and odds are *that* awesome.

Suddenly I envisioned spending the next six months feeling like this and decided there was no way I could. Over the course of treatment, I discovered that I felt worst on the fifth and six days following chemo. Treatment marked the first day in each cycle, so days two and three were the first forty-eight hours after chemo. I started to feel sick on day four with worsening symptoms on days five and six. On the fifth day of the cycle, in addition to feeling like I had the flu, my mouth hurt like when I'd had my wisdom teeth removed. My teeth, gums, and jaw ached like crazy, and anytime I ate, searing pain shot from the back of my mouth across my jaw. By the end of treatment, my mouth pain became so unbearable that I didn't eat on those days, so Dr. Gordon had to prescribe a numbing mouthwash.

My strategy for days five and six became sleeping in late and going to bed early to minimize the number of waking hours I wrestled through in pain. I knew that sounded like a cop-out, and I could imagine lecturing myself that the point of life is not just to get through the bad times. But on my worst days after chemo, the best I could do was sleep. When I couldn't sleep, I had a bunch of books to read, and over Christmas break my dad bought me a TV for passing the time. Often on days five and six I woke up from one to three in the morning, watched a movie or read for a couple of hours, and then fell back asleep for as long as I could. Never before had I slept at least eight hours a night, especially not ten to twelve hours. My body discovered sleep after years of over-committing and spreading myself too thin, and it liked it.

With each chemo cycle, day seven turned the tide. I still felt sick but not incapacitated as on days five and six. Day eight was always the first solid day I felt well. And by "well," I mean *mostly* normal. From day eight until my next treatment seven days later, I felt well enough to go about everyday life, albeit weaker and less energetic than usual. I could eat regularly, and since I didn't eat much the week after chemo, I ate whatever I wanted the second week leading up to my next treatment.

Best of all, I didn't gain any weight because I essentially starved one week and lived like a glutton the next. When people gave me cookie bouquets, cupcakes, or candy, I saved the treats for my second week after chemo in which I gladly indulged my sweet tooth after eating minimally for a week. I think my stomach knew I was about to ignore it for a week, so it wanted to store up, like a bear before hibernation, and that worked well. The only problem with this eating plan came after chemo ended and I felt great every day so my stomach kept demanding cake and cookies.

My first day five (a.k.a. when I hit the wall) fell on Monday, a Wheaton-sanctioned reading day set aside to prepare for exams. After a full weekend, I had counted on that day to finish my papers and study. Day six fell on Tuesday, the day of my Drugs and Society exam and the due date for those two papers. Luckily, I had already turned in one paper the previous week and had studied a few hours for my Drugs and Society exam. While lying in bed, I typed what I could, and then I emailed my other two professors in whose classes I had papers due. Dr. Cohick said I could email her my Corinthians paper when I made it home to Texas, and Dr. Lundin gave me a full semester's extension on my Senior Seminar capstone paper and literature major portfolio. If that wasn't enough grace, I was about to receive even more.

On Tuesday morning, I woke up for my exam and felt absolutely terrible. It was day six, one of the worst two days of my chemo cycle, but I didn't know that at the time so couldn't plan around exams accordingly. I threw on the first clothes I found, arrived to class, and immediately collapsed into a desk. Head in my hands, it was all I could do not to sprawl out on the classroom's cold tile floor. My teammate Kelli and friend Maggie came over and told me to ask the professor for grace. Now, I went on to be a teacher, so it's not that I'm intimidated by them, but I rarely asked my teachers or professors for help. I figured if I wasn't ready for an exam or finished with a paper, no matter how busy I was, I could have done something about it. I didn't want to ask someone else to help fix my mistake. On this day, however, I knew I'd have to get over my aversion to asking for help.

When Dr. Eggimann arrived, she must have noticed that I looked less than prime because she asked what was up. I asked if we could talk outside, and knowing I'd just undergone my first chemotherapy treatment, she said yes but needed a minute to pass out the exams. I walked into the hallway, and when she joined me, I turned around, summoned up all my courage, and blurted out, "There's no possible way I can pass this exam right now," exhaling quickly. I explained that I had studied, so I didn't lack preparation, but I felt like crawling into bed and taking a bottle of sleeping pills to make this terrible day disappear. Without hesitation, Dr. Eggimann said I didn't have to take the exam right then; she would let my mom proctor it for me from home. Surprised and grateful, I said, "I'm not sure if I'm allowed to do this, but can I hug you?" She smiled and nodded, so I gave her a big hug. I mean, what kind of professor lets a college student take an exam a thousand miles away at home with her mom as a proctor?

Floored by her grace and trust in my integrity, I felt affirmed that Wheaton was right where I needed to be. I tucked that experience away as a lesson for my future teaching days—that I might respond to students with grace and trust equal to what my professors showed me, rather than my go-to attitude of cynicism and doubt. I left the exam and made it back to my college house, crawling back into bed, an action becoming more and more routine.

ROAD TRIP FROM...YOU KNOW WHERE

My teammate Stef and I planned to begin the fifteen hour drive to Dallas that afternoon, but since I'd been on a downhill slope since Sunday, I hadn't packed a piece of clothing for my three week Christmas break yet. One of my Kanakuk co-counselors from the previous summer also attended Wheaton, and when Laura asked if she could stop by, I said yes. Little did she know she would end up packing for me while I reclined on my futon. She pulled out t-shirts, asking which ones I wanted to pack and making sure I had matching shorts to go with. Then she went through my closet, holding up item after item like a personal assistant. I couldn't even rouse myself to throw some t-shirts into a bag and go, so I greatly appreciated Laura's willingness to do whatever it took to serve me.

A few hours later, Stef and I pulled away from Wheaton, ready for our last road trip together. Over the previous three years, we'd made the trip to and from Texas numerous times, and she was an ideal partner for a fifteen hour drive. We liked the same music, we both had an unspoken commitment to staying awake while the other person drove, and though we engaged in meaningful conversation, neither of us felt pressure to fill periods of silence. Our road trip playlist always kicked off with us singing "Leaving Town" as we pulled away and hit the road. This trip began on day six of my chemo cycle, so I felt flu-like, but I put on my best poker face, trying to reassure Stef that I'd be fine.

We planned to drive eight hours to Joplin, Missouri, but as we drove south through Illinois, the weather wasn't cooperating. Driving through snow is one thing, but driving through a combination of ice, snow, freezing rain, dense fog, and regular rain added some time to our drive. By 5 p.m. we should have passed through St. Louis, but instead we were at least an hour and a half away. We called our teammate Mallory who was ahead of us, and she kept us posted on her slow progress home near the St. Louis suburbs. Mallory told us if the weather was too bad, we could stop and spend the night at her house. We initially turned down the offer, but when we saw people sliding off the road and Mallory called us back from the ditch she'd veered into, we opted to stop at her parents' house for the night, way behind our goal.

It didn't matter whether I drove or rode shotgun; either way, I felt terrible. On top of it being day six, I had a sinus infection, and I had begun taking birth control pills because the doctors said they might potentially protect against infertility due to chemo. But the pills only added to the nausea I already felt from treatment, so I stopped taking them after that day. For my sake and Stef's, I knew we needed to stop. Mallory's mom welcomed us into her home, gave me ibuprofen, found a humidifier to help with my sinus infection, and tucked me right into bed.

What should have been a fourteen and a half hour drive to my house in north Dallas ended up taking eighteen hours. Usually Stef and I drove an equal portion of the trip, but this time, of the eighteen hours, I drove around three and a half. It was all I could do to keep things together, but Stef carried on, uncomplaining—even when I tried eating a Subway sandwich but promptly threw it up. Stef didn't even wince; she patted my back, asked if I was okay, and rolled down the window. Despite all of the backcountry roads I'd driven to Kanakuk through the Ozark mountains, I had never once experienced motion sickness, especially not while riding shotgun on a smooth highway.

When we finally made it to my house north of Dallas, relief flooded over me like never before. Thinking we'd have one last great session on the road together, I'd had high hopes for our final drive, but it turned out to be a nightmare. I felt even worse for Stef because she still had four more hours until she made it home to the suburbs of Houston. Her parents unpacked her stuff from my car, loaded it into their Rav 4, and headed south for The Woodlands. Back inside my house, I couldn't even make it upstairs to my room. I walked through the front door, made a beeline for the couch, and fell into the cushions, exhausted, feeling terrible, and hoping the next six months wouldn't be like this.

EXPECTATIONS

Here's the thing: side effects suck. It's like, *Hey, to add insult to the injury that you have cancer and could die, let's make sure you feel terrible in the process, too.* I felt completely fine until I underwent chemo. While I realize that's not always the case—many people have ailments that uncover their cancer—treatment as a "good thing" wasn't always easy to grasp.

Awareness is half the battle. The shock of how terrible I felt on that first day five during exam week came because I felt okay the first forty-eight hours after treatment. Everyone had warned me about days two and three, so I adequately feared them, but when they passed better than expected, I figured chemo wasn't so bad. Then days four, five, and six hit, and my great expectations quickly dissipated. I'm a little bit of a cynic (though underneath every cynic is a little ray of hope), so I like to have low expectations in life. Call me a pessimist, tell me I should have more joy, and chide me for taking the easy way out; I know. Nevertheless, I think I go with the flow fairly easily because I have those low expectations. In my view, if you live with high expectations, you'll only be disappointed, but if you have low expectations, you just might be pleasantly surprised.

That mantra helped me immensely with teaching high school. Professors, friends, and other teachers repeated over and over how difficult my first year of teaching would be. They made it sound as if every day would be a struggle, I'd question why I'd chosen the profession, and more or less, I'd hate my life. Effectively terrified and expecting life to be awful, I headed into my first teaching job with not just low, but the worst expectations. At graduation the following June, I sat in my always ridiculous-looking cap, gown, and hood with the other teachers, reflecting on the year. It hadn't been terrible. In fact, I realized, I'd actually enjoyed it! I loved my students, I had a great ministry, and my teaching only improved each day. There were difficult days to be sure, but those days never made me hate life. Now, teaching two months after finishing chemo may have impacted my perspective on what "difficult" actually means, but still; all those people had prepared me for the worst, and with those expectations, I was immensely and pleasantly surprised.

My point? I'm glad I expected cancer treatment to be painful (I just wish I hadn't gotten overconfident after those not-so-bad days two and three). While chemo wasn't fun, I did have better days than others, and I still had blessings I could claim. I think expecting that treatment would set me back and take some of the wind out of my sails helped prepare me. If I'd expected to sail through treatment without a hitch, my bad days probably would've felt much worse. When we expect that the journey through trials might not be fun, I think we'll find ourselves pleasantly surprised when we wake up and have those unexpected good days.

SIDE EFFECTS

My doctors gave me a list of side effects to look for, but they explained that every person reacts differently to chemo. Some people feel worst with the very first chemo treatment and improve each session, while others fare better at the start only to slowly feel the cumulative effects of chemo as the process wears on. Doctors warned me about hair loss, mouth sores, nausea, brittle finger and toe nails, skin that could develop sores or become super dry, and many other potential issues, so I at least had a general list of symptoms to expect. I needed to understand what hazards I faced to effectively deal with them. I only wish I had taken a more long-term view of side effects from the start so that, a few years later when my toes still fall asleep while I'm standing, I know that's normal.

I always figured side effects were part and parcel of having cancer, until my mom's cousin sent me the story of a guy who also had Hodgkin's. He mentioned that while he always prayed for healing, he never thought to pray for minimal side effects. I had never thought about that either. I was challenged by the fact that I tended to pray safe prayers. I mean, I definitely prayed for miraculous healing, but since my outlook was pretty good, I mostly prayed to avoid major hitches. I prayed that I would make it through side effects and be able to deal with them, and those are good prayers.

However, I never thought about praying a big prayer for, say, zero side effects. At first that sounded crazy—after all, side effects seemed inevitable, like they came with the territory. But I realized that praying "crazy" prayers for zero side effects meant I would have to trust that God could actually accomplish them. I knew in my head that God *could* do miracles like saving my hair or keeping me from throwing up, but I feared

He might not, so I never prayed that way. Convicted about my small, pansy prayers, I decided to start praying more boldly.

My view of prayer has grown over the years, and I like to think of it through an analogy of playing cards. I used to think prayer meant saying, "Lord, deal me the right hand," but now I think it's more like saying, "Lord, give me the strength and courage to trust You with whatever hand You deal me." Often in my life, prayer ends up changing my heart and understanding of God more than it changes my circumstances. With that changed heart, I usually end up viewing my situation differently, trusting God is the dealer and knows what He's doing.

We need to pray radically—whether for zero side effects, for our trials to come to a grinding halt, or whatever else the situation requires— trusting that God is big enough to answer those prayers. He did create the universe, after all. But ultimately, we have to surrender to Him however the circumstances play out, echoing David's claim in Psalm 31:15, "My times are in Your hands, Lord." Though I lowered my expectations for how I'd feel over the course of treatment after this first chemo and its miserable aftermath, I learned to raise my expectations for what God could do.

In the Word:

- **Psalm 38** (excerpts) "My back is filled with searing pain; there is no health in my body. I am feeble and utterly crushed; I groan in anguish of heart. All my longings lie open before You, O Lord; my sighing is not hidden from You. My heart pounds, my strength fails me; even the light has gone from my eyes.... I wait for You, O Lord; You will answer, O Lord my God.... For I am about to fall and my pain is ever with me.... O Lord, do not forsake me; be not far from me, O my God. Come quickly to help me, O Lord my Savior."
- **Psalm 68:19-20** "Praise be to the Lord, to God our Savior, who daily bears our burdens. Our God is a God who saves; from the Sovereign Lord comes escape from death."
- **Psalm 86:7** "In the day of my trouble I will call to You, for You will answer me."
- **Psalm 102:1-2** "Hear my prayer, O Lord; let my cry for help come to You. Do not hide Your face from me when I am in distress. Turn Your ear to me; when I call, answer me quickly."

Other Resources:

- The National Coalition for Cancer Survivorship, or NCCS, (www.canceradvocacy.org) has a helpful website and a mobile app with information on a variety of topics: policy, financial issues, end of life, living with cancer, etc. The website has a section called the "Cancer Survival Toolbox" with help on communication, information, decisions, rights, and other subjects for patients.
- Lindi Skin (www.lindiskin.com) has skin care products for cancer patients. My kit came with moisturizing body lotion, lavender and citrus face serum, face moisturizer, face wash, body wash, and face tint. I loved them because skin feels different, can take on new sensitivities, and can even look a different hue during treatment.

- The National Cancer Institute (www.cancer.gov) has many free and helpful publications. Two workbooks entitled "Chemotherapy and You" and "Radiation and You" provide detailed information about possible side effects of treatment, ways to cope with everything from infertility to dry mouth and nausea, and places to write down answers to questions you have for your oncologist. Find and follow the link for NCI Publications and browse the various options to order resources.

CHAPTER 4

With a Little Help from My Friends

Sunday, January 4, 2009

"The LORD is faithful to all His promises and loving toward all He has made" (Psalm 145:13b).

Happy New Year! Sorry it's been a while, but I hope y'all had blessed Christmas and New Year's celebrations! We've enjoyed the holidays here in Fairview, and even more than the time to rest, I was thrilled with the 80 degree weather we had yesterday. In January. That's amazing (although, of course, it's 43 degrees right now. All good things must come to an end).

Anyway, how about a recap of the past week or so? I had my second treatment on Wednesday (Christmas Eve) in Dallas. It was definitely a different experience than my treatment at Northwestern in Chicago, but it was such a blessing to get on the schedule, especially on Christmas Eve. The doctor was... very frank...but he gave my dad, my friend Caroline, and me something to laugh about. Treatment happened, and I felt great on Christmas, which is a huge praise! Thanks for so many prayers! I got a little tired, but then again, at one point, about five of us McGinnis cousins were sleeping on my grandparents' couches, so it's hard to say whether my fatigue was isolated to chemo or not. The day after Christmas I also felt pretty well; again, I was just a little tired physically—or maybe drained is a better word, since it's not like I was falling asleep at meals or anything.

Then the bad days five and six hit, and they weren't so much fun. Since Tuesday, I've been much less sedentary, which is nice for a change. For my parents' twenty-sixth anniversary on New Year's Day, they took us out *with* them, and it was nice to be at our favorite restaurant together. Everywhere we go, it seems as if we run into someone who is praying for us, or we meet someone who has an encouraging word or knows someone else who's had Hodgkin's. Our waiter at Roy's had a best friend years ago who survived it and is doing great. It's crazy how so many people know Hodgkin's survivors because it's a rare form of cancer, and before this, we knew nothing about it at all. But, God is good like that and has provided encouragement in huge and unexpected ways.

All I have left to say is how thankful I am for a sovereign God who truly loves us. When I felt bad on the worst days after treatment, my mom came up and literally put me to bed, tucking me in and praying for me. Seeing how much it pains my parents when I'm just feeling *bad* has totally put things in perspective. I can't tell you why bad things happen (I mean, I could give you a great explanation of sin and so on, but you know what I mean). I *can*, however, tell you that, just as my parents love me so greatly that they can't bear watching me writhe in pain, the Father loves us even more. He created us, and when my mom broke down while tucking me into bed this past week, I saw a picture of how hard it is for Him to see us suffer and struggle.

He is our Father, and just as it hurts my parents when I'm in pain, He loves us even more. That may seem like common sense to y'all, but there's something about seeing your parents suffer over your pain that's made God's love more real to me. Anyway, He is good. One of the Psalms I read speaks about His goodness, saying, "Praise Him for His acts of power; praise Him for His surpassing greatness" (Psalm 150:2), and we have absolutely seen those so far in this—not only can we praise Him for all the things He's *done* but so much more for who He *is* and His surpassing greatness.

Thank you again! One round down, five more to go! Have a blessed week!

On Christ the solid Rock I stand,

Hannah
Posted at 2:27 p.m.

THE HAPPIEST CHRISTMAS

Despite having just gone through the worst road trip ever, my condition started to improve. I didn't know at the time that day seven of my two week chemo cycle was the day I turned a corner. The morning after Stef and I made it home to Texas, I woke up still feeling under the weather but at least not like a semi truck had run me over. The day continued to improve, and each day afterward was better than the one before...at least until my next treatment. I actually enjoyed the week leading up to Christmas reasonably well. The doctors wanted me to keep chemo treatments fourteen days apart, give or take a day if necessary, so my second treatment fell on Thursday, December 25th. Since no one administered chemo on Christmas, my options were Christmas Eve or the 26th. We didn't want to fly back to Chicago right before or after Christmas, so Dr. Gordon referred us to an oncologist he'd met who practiced in Dallas. Coincidentally (or as more evidence of God's great plan), my friend Caroline used to be neighbors with the Dallas doctor.

Trying to schedule that chemo was crazy; however, on December 23rd, the hospital in Dallas called to let me know I was on the schedule for chemo the following day. Because she went to college in Texas and couldn't physically support me at school, and since she vaguely knew the doctor, Caroline assured me she wanted to come with me to treatment. When I reminded her that she'd be spending four hours in a hospital on Christmas Eve and she didn't exactly have the best track record around medical procedures, Caro didn't care. She was coming whether I liked it or not, and I'm so glad she came. It was...an experience. The oncologist's first words upon entering the room were, "Well, this is the most difficult thing you've ever faced." *Hi, nice to meet you, too. And Merry Christmas, by the way,* I wanted to say.

He asked me how old I was, and upon hearing me say twenty-one, he scratched his chin as he mumbled, Absentminded-Professor-style, "Hmm...yes...well...Yep, this is the most difficult thing you've ever faced," as if he had to run through all possible difficulties I could have faced at my age and concluded by agreeing with his initial assessment. I looked around at Caroline and my dad and saw mortified expressions on their faces. At least I wasn't the only one taken aback.

The situation only grew in amusement from there. He proceeded to tell me I was lucky all my hair hadn't fallen out yet. He said, "You know, your scalp's just going to itch and burn and *wham!* All your hair is going to fall out."

Wanting to give him the benefit of my growing doubt in his bedside manner, I casually replied, "Yeah...I'm not looking forward to that."

The doctor responded, "Well, you could be dead."

True, but seriously?!? "I tell myself that every day," I countered, nodding my head and trying my best to look sincere as I squelched a laugh. As soon as we left the hospital, Caroline, my dad, and I erupted in laughter as we debated whether he'd been serious or was attempting to joke around. I think the verdict's still out on that one.

I felt out of sorts that afternoon, but since chemo didn't hit me hardest until days five and six, I knew I would at least be okay that night and on Christmas. We skipped Christmas Eve services at church and instead hung out as a family at home. On Christmas morning, my family delayed our annual present opening extravaganza so I could sleep in and take all of my post-chemo medications slowly. When I finished the morning routine, my sisters and I headed downstairs and assumed our regular places around the room before opening presents. My dad huddled us up and prayed, thanking the Lord for family, for being together on Christmas, and for the gift of His Son.

That Christmas was the sweetest one we've ever spent together. No one was impatient, no one rushed off to use new gifts, and no one took long naps after presents. Instead, we hung out in our family room, so thankful we were together. Cancer changes things. No matter what type or stage of cancer someone has, it has the ability to refocus perspective and make the things that matter so much more important while making trivial things even less significant. We felt that on Christmas. We didn't really care what we had received, but we were acutely aware that it was good for all of us to be alive, that we had so much to be grateful for, and that family was a huge blessing.

At our extended family gathering that night, the feeling persisted. We circled up and my aunts, uncles, cousins, and grandparents took turns lifting my family and me up in prayer. God has blessed me greatly with a wonderful extended family, and though we don't always take the time to be intentional or show our weaknesses to each other, we shared something very authentic that night.

Over the final two weeks of Christmas break, many friends wanted to meet with me, catch up, and see how I was doing. I had lunch with some Kanakuk friends I'd worked with the previous few summers, and my friend Sarah-Graham asked me if the support had been overwhelming—whether in a good or bad way. I mulled over her question and realized that so far, it *had* been a little overwhelming, but definitely in a good way. I was overwhelmed by the goodness of God's people in this time, something I hadn't expected. I figured people would either nosily pry or awkwardly avoid me, but I was endlessly blessed by people and humbled by the importance of community during life's trials.

LETTING OTHERS KNOW

I saw early on in my journey with cancer that we have to let others join us in our trials. We'll be a mess and things won't always be pretty, so our pride and vanity might take a hit as people see us through our lows. But if you experience a fraction of what I did walking through cancer, you'll be grateful for letting others in.

Patients have their own decisions to make in so many areas, and figuring out who to tell and how to let people know about cancer is one of those. I've known people who didn't tell others about their diagnosis because they wanted to maintain privacy, and I can understand that desire for anonymity. However, at the end of the day, I can't imagine keeping people in the dark about my cancer for a number of reasons.

First of all, there have been a couple of times when my mom and dad have had cancer scares—they've gone in for a biopsy due to a lump, found a spot of basal cell carcinoma, or been told to monitor something. Each time, I'm incredulous at their failure to tell me such information. It's only been after the fact, when they've received the "all clear," that they've passed on the tiny detail that a doctor was concerned about the possibility of cancer. I always get angry then ask why that somehow slipped their minds, and they say they didn't want to worry me. When I counter that I would have been praying for them, they've said, "I figured if I had cancer, I had cancer, and if I didn't, I didn't. So, I would let you know only when I did." Yes, this from my parents who were absolute prayer warriors, rallying any and all of their acquaintances to pray for me during my battle.

Sometimes trials may not seem important to share, but if you found out a close friend or family member kept a struggle or cancer scare from you to protect you, wouldn't you be frustrated? I was, and as I anticipate my parents persisting in their stubbornness as they age, I will continue to be frustrated with their selective amnesia regarding cancer scares. One of these lapses in communication occurred right before one of my post-chemo CT scans, and I made sure to ask my parents how they'd feel if I received the results that my cancer returned, but, so as not to worry anyone, I simply omitted that detail. Their pointed looks told me they might disown me for even thinking such a horrible thing. I'm hoping they got my point.

By letting others in, we give them an opportunity to serve us and find practical ways of dealing with traumatic events in both our lives and theirs. What a sad case it would be to let others know when it's too late for them to pray for healing and too late for us to receive encouragement and be blessed by those God has placed in our lives.

THE BEST THERAPY I RECEIVED

Secondly, I firmly believe that by telling others, I was efficient. I've learned that people find out things about each other even when they haven't seen them in years. I figured my news would probably get around, and instead of being on the defensive by answering the same questions a million times over, it would be better if I just attacked things head-on by letting people know. Unaware of CaringBridge and other official patient websites, I remembered my college roommate Lisa had a blog while spending a semester in Africa, so I found her site, signed up for my own, and began to write.

At first, I was hesitant to blog because I didn't want to be another self-important voice adding to the noise of blogs and Internet publishing. It seemed a little presumptuous to think everyone out there wanted to read and learn all about me (imagine my hesitance to write a book...). Despite my reluctance, I was won over after mass-texting the same things again and again to my friends, family members, campers, and other acquaintances. I didn't want blogging to replace individual or personal contact, so I encouraged friends to still text, email, and feel free to ask questions. Blogging allowed me to summarize my updates and then people had a blanket of understanding before asking follow-up questions.

Additionally, writing was significantly therapeutic. Maybe it's because I already have an affinity for writing, but blogging helped me. Most of the time, I was busy answering questions, going to appointments, staying on top of life, and otherwise trying to avoid really having to think about everything going on. It's challenging enough to deal with the side effects, stress, and other struggles that come with cancer, so it was hard to process my situation because I didn't *want* to deal with it. However, when I wrote, I realized that I actually had to assess my current condition.

People always asked me how I was doing and I answered to the best of my ability, but only when I sat down to write did I really have to grapple with my situation and emotions. Sometimes I'd sit down and surprisingly discover, *Wow, I'm doing pretty well right now!* and other times I'd start writing and realize everything weighed on me. I found that it was more significant for my testimony to remain honest about my state, whether full of trust or doubt, than to try and sound lofty or super positive.

Blogging isn't for everyone and maybe CaringBridge sounds downright morbid—my teammate's mom said that exact thing about her reluctance to join a site. Regardless of people's instincts toward those things, I still encourage them to write. As Socrates said, "The unexamined life is not worth living." We don't have to think about cancer or our difficulties every second of the day; in fact, we probably want to avoid that very thing, and rightly so. However, to avoid ever processing how we're *really* doing is to avoid the elephant in the room. The fact of the matter was I had cancer, so I was honest about that. Denying it definitely wouldn't heal me.

Having a written record of our thoughts and feelings during trials can be incredibly helpful down the road—I've learned that over the years through writing down some of my prayers. I love looking back and seeing the ways God has answered prayers, healed my heart, and handled each situation with sovereignty. Just like with a prayer journal, being able to look back and see from what depths of physical pain, emotional trial, and spiritual struggle He brought me during cancer has helped me since then. Trying to accurately recapture my emotions and thoughts after the fact would have been really difficult, and I probably wouldn't have gotten around to it. I'm a definite proponent for finding something through which we can record how we're doing—an old journal, a website, or any other means of written communication—and starting to chronicle our fears, pains, joys, and even the fact that we might not *want* to think about the trial at hand. It will be a blessing down the road.

DON'T GO IT ALONE FOR OUR SAKES

People always ask me about the greatest lesson I encountered during cancer. I don't even have to think about my answer. The biggest blessing was by far seeing the goodness of God's people. I had to rely on the Lord daily to make it through, and He sustained me by providing incredible support all around.

More than four years later, I still find people who read my blog and prayed for me that I never knew about. Surprisingly (as a cynic), I never felt angry at people for their pity or sympathy, but instead, I was thankful for every bit of support I received. I went to a close-knit, private preparatory school from kindergarten through twelfth grade, and we always chided the "Trinity Grapevine" that didn't let a single piece of news go untouched. More times than I could count, I'd rolled my eyes at mothers who had to talk, students who knew everything about everyone, and the lack of anonymity there. However, my attitude toward the grapevine changed completely when I received my diagnosis.

My mom taught at the school, and she passed on my prayer request as I began my tests. Word got around, and she eventually emailed all teachers and assistants asking for prayer. That message reached the school counselor who added it to the official prayer request list. The list eventually made it into an all-school email, a message to all parents, faculty and staff, and alumni. Within days, I had a vast network of prayer support from Trinity Christian Academy and company. People I hadn't talked to since graduation four years prior sent me Facebook messages, passed on names of college friends who'd had cancer, and let me know they were praying faithfully. The very thing I so hated while at the school was an incredible blessing in my time of need. Weeks before if I had thought about everyone from my high school knowing my business, I would have cringed. It's funny how God changes our hearts and often uses unexpected means to bless us in our trials.

My mom's kindergarten classes made me a chemo countdown poster with my picture and the number of treatments I had on it. With each successive treatment, the class would place a smiley face over that number, count down the remaining treatments, and cheer loudly for me. A couple of times I called my mom after treatment and she took the phone into her classroom. I listened as she announced that I finished another treatment. Each time, those kids' eruption of joy brought me to tears, reminding me that even five year olds who I'd never met were blessings as they prayed daily for me with their sweet, childlike faith. If you'd told me ahead of time kindergarteners would be my fiercest prayer warriors, I would have politely said, "Oh, that's precious" and forgotten about it. However, during my cancer journey, I came to rely on those five year olds and their faithful prayers for "Miss Hannah McGinnis," and I am still so grateful for and humbled by their love. Even today, I still get teary eyed when I think about how encouraging people were as they helped me survive the trial.

SHARING THE BURDEN

I learned to be unafraid in asking for help and sharing my needs. My mom always says she's good at a lot of things, but she absolutely can't read people's minds. So, it was a pretty safe bet that when I went through cancer, people *really* couldn't read my mind, but more often than not, they wanted to help. I started explaining to friends and family members what I needed, whether help with my chores, daily encouragement, a friend to come sit and watch TV with me, or someone to pack my suitcase. In even the most menial of tasks and efforts, my friends could tangibly bless me in my difficulty.

With a few friends, at times I'd felt as if I was carrying more than just my share of our relationship. But when I had cancer, I was forced to take a break, rest, and receive love. In that new season, I was overwhelmed with love. Where I could no longer carry the relationship, most of my friends picked up the slack, and our relationships today are so much deeper because I had to rely on them to carry our friendship for a while. I'm fairly cynical, and all too often I expect people to fail. While saying "Thank you for restoring my faith in humankind" seemed a bit too cliché and straight from a Christmas movie, there *is* a little truth to every cliché. We were created for community, and I was changed by remembering that and leaning on other believers. Daily I saw the goodness of God's people, which ultimately helped me remember how good *God* is and how great is His love for us. God can do amazing things in our hearts and lives if we'll receive help from others. If we let them in, we can prepare to be blessed by the manifestation of Christ's love through mere man.

My club volleyball experience is a great example of what was, to me, a whimsical decision to invite a friend along but in the end was clearly God providentially providing someone to help bear my burdens. I signed on to coach a 14-and-under girls' club volleyball team in November while my many doctor visits commenced. I figured if I was going to spend five to six hours a week in a gym at practice and ten weekends at tournaments in random gyms around Chicago, I might as well recruit a teammate to help me and add some fun. Sure, I'd be cutting my measly monthly coaching salary in half, but I figured the fun I'd have coaching with a friend would be worth it. When I ran through my different teammates, I immediately thought of one of the freshmen, Brooke. She didn't seem like one to wince at the thought of coaching fourteen year old girls or giving up a couple nights a week plus some weekends to coach. When I called her to ask if she'd like to help out, without any hesitation she said she was game, and I knew we would have a ton of fun.

When my diagnosis came out a few weeks later, I sat Brooke down and told her she might have to be more than my assistant. Now we needed to be co-coaches, making equally weighted decisions. I told her she could back out and my feelings wouldn't be hurt. After all, she'd signed on to assist who she thought was her healthy senior captain who would take the lead. While I knew Brooke would do a great job in my absence, I wasn't sure how comfortable *she'd* feel with the idea.

I should have known nothing daunts Brooke; she rolls with the punches. She said she would still coach with me, and though I planned out most practices, I had to miss three in a row during the first month of our season because of all the medical tests I underwent in December. Later, I missed a few more practices and one tournament when I wasn't feeling well. That meant Brooke had to find a car, make the frozen twenty-five mile drive to the gym, and manage ten fourteen year old girls by herself. Though I love my other teammates and have deep bonds with them, I can't imagine having anyone other than Brooke as my co-coach. Freshmen couldn't have cars at Wheaton, so other teammates might have freaked out at the pressure and awkwardness of borrowing a car for the night. Others might have worried about driving to practice along an icy route to an unfamiliar suburb without streetlights or effective signs. Still others might have doubted their ability to corral ten middle school girls and maintain focus during the two and a half hour practice. But not Brooke. To each obstacle she *didn't* sign up for, Brooke told me, "No problem," and she meant it.

What was to me a spontaneous decision to invite more fun into my coaching job became an incredible blessing and just a hint of the many ways I would be overwhelmed by unquestioning support during my cancer struggle. Brooke and I had a blast, and she helped me process what I went through. Though today we don't talk all the time, I can pick up with her from exactly where we left off. I only ever played on a team with her for three months, but spending the next seven months coaching together amidst my trial made her like a sister, and my relationship with

Brooke is just one example where I can look back and see that my life is far better because of cancer than it was before.

TANGIBLE BLESSINGS

I'm so thankful for the many friends and family members who asked me what I needed or how they could specifically help me. Just as everyone has different love languages, each person needs support in different ways during trials. I loved most when people were thoughtful. Whether it was my friend Katie texting me, "Thinking of you and praying for you today" faithfully on each of my chemotherapy days, or whether it was my teammates who made a calendar of days five and six and signed up to bring me Jamba Juice and keep me company, all of those thoughtful acts and words encouraged me.

When people ask me about the best thing someone did for me, I can recount endless tales of how others blessed me with their gifts, love, and encouragement. But the chemo care packages I received top the list. My mom has three sisters, and those women are ridiculously gifted in creativity and thoughtfulness, so as soon as I was diagnosed, they came up with a plan. My Aunts Karen, Debi, and Jill decided they would send each person in my family a care package each day I had chemotherapy. Surprised enough at *my* first care package, I was even more astounded that they sent packages to each of my sisters and parents. My aunts realized that as much as I would struggle each time I had chemo (especially being far from home), my parents and sisters would also struggle. I had a sense of impending doom each time chemo day rolled around because before treatment I felt the best I had in fourteen days. All morning long, I dreaded feeling terrible again. But I eagerly awaited the mailman's delivery of my care package before I headed to the hospital. I told my aunts that other than seeing my nurse Michelle, their care packages were the only things I looked forward to on treatment days.

The packages were different every time. My aunts sent books, DVDs, my favorite candy, and random trinkets like an eye mask, an ice pack with a kitten cover, playing cards, and brightly colored socks. For my sixth chemo marking the halfway point in treatment, my aunt sent me party hats, blow horns, and confetti for celebrating. In my first care package, one aunt sent me a packet of fifteen bracelets. They were fun and colorful, and she thought I could give them to my friends as reminders to pray for me. I had fifteen bracelets and fourteen teammates, so I gave each teammate one. They put them on when I gave them out, but I didn't know if the girls would actually wear the bracelets. Months later, when I passed different teammates on campus, I was surprised to see them still wearing the thin, colorful bracelets as a reminder to pray and sign of solidarity.

My aunts' thoughtfulness is by far one of the most unique and helpful things anyone did to make my cancer experience better. Whether they sent frivolous trinkets and fun toys or thoughtful books and prayer bracelets, my aunts reminded me that, though others might have moved on with their lives and forgotten that another chemo day was upon me, my aunts had not. They were still with me, and though they were in Texas and Colorado, they were emotionally supporting and tangibly blessing me.

DON'T GO IT ALONE FOR THEIR SAKES

Often, I think people wanted to help and support me, but they didn't know how or what to say. Should they ask me about it? Or would I be sick of answering questions? Should they avoid the topic? Or would that be weird since I still had cancer even if they didn't mention it? How would I react—would I laugh, cry, be depressed, be weak, or look like a shell of my former self?

While the road I traveled dealing with cancer was really challenging, I never anticipated that others might struggle with my diagnosis as well.

They didn't always know what to say, so when they said the wrong thing, I gave them some grace...and then kindly taught them that certain things were better to say than others. I learned that if we take some time to help others process by allowing their questions, making them feel at ease rather than awkward, and letting them join with us in our trials, there's a good chance we'll help them as much as they assist us.

I'm eternally grateful for the support of friends who took time out of their busy lives to sit with me through different appointments, biopsies, treatments, and even follow-up check-ups years later. I never once went to chemotherapy alone; Mr. or Mrs. Armstrong was always there, one of my parents came to every other treatment, and I always had a teammate or friend along. While their support helped me, I think it also helped them to feel useful, get a better understanding of what was happening, and process the situation.

Early on during my tests, my mom and my Wheaton volleyball coach Jen impressed upon me the idea that sometimes, others needed to help me more than I actually needed it. I appreciated my teammates' repeated offers to come to appointments and chemotherapy with me, but there were times when the tests were elementary so I honestly didn't *need* someone to come. When I called my mom and explained that people wanted to go to routine appointments with me, she helped me understand that sometimes, whether I needed a friend there or not, the other person might need it in order to wrap his or her head around the situation. Jen added that sometimes letting others help is the only way they can feel useful and able to serve in incomprehensible times. Their words gave me a totally new perspective, and I was thereafter blessed because I let people join me.

Sometimes, though *we* may be okay, *others* struggle to process our situations. My diagnosis was hard on my wide-eyed freshmen teammates who saw their senior captain facing a difficult trial. At that point in life, college students usually feel free, indestructible, and unburdened by things like cancer. I learned to let them in, and when they offered to come with me if I needed, I was tempted to say they shouldn't take time out of their busy schedules for something routine. But when my friends joined me, they could physically support me, and I think that allowed them to make sense of what was happening so much better.

We need to let others help us amidst trials, not just for our sakes but for *their* sakes, too. Now, I don't mean that patronizingly, as if to say, "Well, I'll be so benevolent and lower myself by allowing you to come along so that I can condescend to help ye lowly beings." I definitely needed support and encouragement during cancer. Instead, I realized the people around me struggled with my challenges in a completely different way than I did, but the trial could be just as impactful in their lives as in mine.

ALLOWING FOR BLESSINGS

If you've ever received money from other believers—whether they're paying for your meal, sending you on a mission trip, or just helping you—you might have heard the old Christian saying, "Don't rob me of this opportunity to bless you." What are you supposed to say to that? They just pulled the ultimate trump card because there's no way you can reject their offer after throwing down that line. No one would venture to answer, "No, I insist *I* pay and thus rob you of God's call to bestow His blessing on me."

Though that line can be highly annoying and conversation-stalling, there is truth to it. While cancer was an intense journey and there was no requirement to share each moment of it with everyone in my life, I had to embrace the irritating yet truthful "opportunity to bless" statement. We can't rob a friend or family member of an opportunity to aid us when they otherwise might feel utterly helpless with how to minister to us. Though it might be humbling and difficult, it will be worthwhile to take others along on the journey.

I'm pretty independent. If my finishing college in Chicago during cancer doesn't illustrate the point, note that I moved across the ocean to Hawaii on my own after graduation to teach high school English. I can take care of myself, and though I love people and am energized by spending time with them, I do okay on my own as well. When I was in high school, too often I compared my relationship with the Lord to those around me, and I had to remind myself over and over to fix my eyes on Him alone. In addition, I had high expectations of people, but they would repeatedly let me down. When those things happened, I thought, *Okay, Lord, it's You and me, just You and me,* only reinforcing my ardent independence. Now, there is definite truth to that statement: at some level, it *is* just about our individual relationship with the Lord.

However, going through cancer dramatically changed my understanding of my relationship with God. Yes, it's me and the Lord first and foremost, but He placed me on this earth surrounded by people *not* so I can live as an island. The command is to fix our eyes on God alone (Hebrews 12:2), but He's placed people in our lives for a reason. Yes, we will fail each other, and yes, relationships will be difficult. However, when we walk in fellowship with other believers as we keep our eyes fixed on the Lord, the journey will be so much sweeter.

On a difficult day following treatment, three of my best friends came over to hang out with me, and one of them was particularly energetic and talkative. My friend Mallory turned to her and said, "Hey, I think maybe Hannah wants it quieter and calmer right now." I shot her a knowing look, thankful that she apparently read my mind. I appreciated friends who could tell when I needed time and space, but when others couldn't, I tried to be more assertive in asking for time alone. When I needed peace and quiet, I learned to claim it unapologetically. I had to remind myself, *I have cancer, remember? I think they'll understand.* I always joked about pulling "the cancer card," but I rarely used that as an excuse. My mom observed that sometimes those who have the most right to pull some sort of card are usually the least to actually do so. However, a couple of times, I accepted my limits, chalking them up to cancer.

I had to set boundaries to have time and space for myself, but I couldn't go so far as to isolate myself in a time when God could do wonderful things in and through those around me. Our stories and testimonies as we walk through cancer—or any struggle in life, really—are often about more than just the lessons *we* learn. Sometimes those around us will learn and grow more from watching us in a trial than we personally will. Some friends said my story positively impacted a mutual friend who struggled in her walk with the Lord, and I felt overwhelmed by that one day. I realized if God wanted to use this in my life to impact her, cancer would totally be worth it.

Our stories could be life-changing for those around us, and we may never know it. Whether we ever see that fruit or not, we need to let others in on our journey because truthfully, it's not all about us. God will use any means necessary to bring people to Him.

I DIDN'T SIGN UP FOR THIS

Now, maybe my exhortation leaves people thinking this isn't exactly something they signed up for. Occasionally I hear celebrities bemoan the fame that comes with the job. They'll say things like, "Look, I didn't ask to be a role model." That could be true. Most of them probably didn't sign up to be little Suzie's hero. On the other hand, I don't think many people feel too sorry for those celebs. They probably should have known that celebrity brings with it attention, and thus, people will idolize them for their better—or worse—actions.

Cancer was kind of like that (only I think people were more sympathetic to my plight than a millionaire celebrity's). Sometimes I thought, *Wait, I didn't sign up for this!* And other times I asked, *Okay, Lord, couldn't You have grown me through some* other *trial than this?* I mean, I appreciated God thinking I could handle this trial with Him, but still.... Couldn't He have given me some really hard classes or let me struggle through a bad breakup or something?

My cousin Ali told me I was her hero, and I was touched, but when I thought more about it, my cynicism seeped in. *Hero? For what? For not wanting to die? For fighting an invading disease like millions do each day? How does that make me heroic? That's too much pressure!*

We might feel as if this isn't something we signed up for; we didn't choose to be put through this trial. It's nice that others might learn through our struggles, but we didn't choose to be the role model of sorts they look to. We didn't choose to have so much attention fixed on us, and we might not know how or why God is using this trial to teach others.

The hard truth is, for whatever reason, God has allowed us to walk through difficult seasons. If we don't like letting people in or relying on them, it's probably going to be difficult to start amidst a challenging journey. And we very well might be frustrated at the brand of celebrity that comes with something like cancer where everyone wants to know what's going on, how to help, and how we're doing.

We have to see those people not through cynical eyes but instead, with grace and humility, as people wanting—and needing—to help. Rather than feeling ungrateful at the thought of being collateral damage in the process of drawing people to Him, we have to remember it's an honor to be used by God to further His eternal kingdom. And, like those celebrities who drop the ball and have to apologize to fans, if we snap at someone out of pain, respond in frustration rather than love, or are just in a bad mood, it's okay to explain that we're not used to the attention, invasion of privacy, and pain but are working on it.

I learned that even cancer could be a journey that blessed me and deepened relationships if I would let people in, embrace the fact that others might be learning from me, and trust that God didn't fall asleep on the job but rather was doing something purposeful with this disease in and through my life.

In the Word:

- **Psalm 57:1-3** "Have mercy on me, O God, have mercy on me, for in You my soul takes refuge. I will take refuge in the shadow of Your wings until the disaster has passed. I cry out to God Most High, to God, who fulfills His purpose for me. He sends from heaven and saves me, rebuking those who hotly pursue me. God sends His love and His faithfulness."
- **Proverbs 17:17** "A friend loves at all times, and a brother is born for adversity."
- **Philippians 4:10-14** "I rejoice greatly in the Lord that at last you have renewed your concern for me. Indeed, you have been concerned, but you had no opportunity to show it. I am not saying this because I am in need, for I have learned to be content whatever the circumstances. I know what it is to be in need, and I know what it is to have plenty. I have learned the secret of being content in any and every situation, whether well fed or hungry, whether living in plenty or in want. I can do everything through Him who gives me strength. Yet it was good of you to share in my troubles."

On the Web:

- Cancer Support Community (www.cancersupportcommunity. org), formerly Gilda's Club, provides information on cancer support groups, information meetings, exercise classes, and other activities across the country.
- Chemo Angels Cancer Support (www.chemoangels.net) is an organization that my sister Katie heard about at her hospital and signed me up for. Angel Volunteers "adopt" patients undergoing chemotherapy and send cards, occasional small gifts, and other encouragement to their adoptees. Find out how to register as a patient or as a volunteer on their website.
- CaringBridge (www.caringbridge.org) and My Life Line Cancer Foundation (www.mylifeline.org) offer websites for patients to

write and keep friends and family members updated on their journeys.

- Imerman Angels (www.ImermanAngels.org) helps pair cancer fighters and survivors with someone else who has fought the same type of cancer in a mentoring, 1-on-1 connecting program.

CHAPTER 5

Attitude Is Everything

Wednesday, January 14, 2009

"To the LORD I cry aloud, and He answers me from His holy hill. I lie down and sleep; I wake again because the LORD sustains me" (Psalm 3:4-5).

Greetings from the frozen tundra of Wheaton, IL. Tonight's low is -11 degrees, with "wind chill values as low as -31." I kid you not. Needless to say, I will *not* be going outside anytime soon. How convenient to have an actual excuse this winter to avoid the negative temperatures: "I'm sorry, but my weakened immune system simply won't allow me to go outside."

On a different note, I feel like I've learned some things already about how I want to live my life all the time and not just now that I have cancer. Every morning—and especially on days five and six—I literally have to seek the Lord and ask Him to give me the strength to get up, make anything of the day, and sustain me throughout it, and He absolutely has! And yet, having to so physically rely on Him to sustain me has also shown me how often, in life's easier times, I revert back to self-reliance. Sometimes relying on Him can be easier when hard times come than in the everyday routine of life.

Until I really had to start pleading for sustenance throughout the day on a physical level, my prayers were noncommittal and went like, "Lord, give me the strength to go through this day," as I thought about how it wasn't going to be too hard to make it through a day when all I had to worry about was the amount of homework I hadn't done. I've already learned so much about really praying and meaning it when I ask, knowing now how much I really do *need* Him. So, as a fairly independent person, it's been good for me to have to rely on Him each day for physical strength, but it's also something I pray I don't stop doing come May when treatments should end. I have seen so many of His promises be true in ways I hadn't before, such as trusting that He will give me the strength I need. His Word and promises are really alive to me, so that's a huge blessing!

Please pray over the next couple of days for side effects to be nonexistent, that God would give me the strength I need for class and practice tomorrow, and to stay warm! Seriously though, when we went in for treatment on Friday and they took my blood, apparently a part of my white blood cell count was at 150, which is *very* low. I asked my nurse Michelle, "If my white blood cells reach zero, ummm...does that mean I'm dead?" to which she replied, "No," but said obviously my immune system would be *super* low then. So, as the weather outside becomes more frightful and my immune system stays down in the pits, continued prayer against infections or illness would be huge.

I'll close this week's edition of "Hannah McGinnis, Up Close and Personal," with part of this post's title: "I lie down and sleep; I wake again, because the LORD sustains me" (Psalm 3:5). Man, on the nights when I fall into bed and dread feeling bad when I wake up in the morning, this verse is huge. Praise the Lord for redeeming even the laziest of my days when I lie on the couch and watch TV while feeling poorly. Praise Him that His mercies are new each morning and for the promise that He will sustain us when we wake up to face the day.

On Christ the solid Rock I stand,

Hannah
Posted at 5:45 p.m.

BACK TO REALITY (AGAIN)

Christmas break ended all too quickly and soon it was time to make the fifteen hour drive back to Wheaton. Stef needed a few extra days at home over break, so my dad made the long drive back with me instead. We arrived in Chicago on Thursday night, January 8th, and we stayed downtown and saw the musical *Wicked*. On Friday morning, my dad and I woke up and explored the Museum of Science and Industry. My mom couldn't miss school to drive to Chicago with me, so she flew in Friday afternoon right before my third treatment. Both of my parents hung out with me through chemo, but someone needed to take care of my sister Madelyn, so my mom and dad swapped duties.

My dad flew home Saturday morning after chemo and my mom stayed with me. She helped me get through day two and the start of day three, unpack from Christmas break, and prepare me for my final semester of college. On Sunday morning we went to breakfast with her friend Sandy, and afterwards she took my mom to the airport so she could get home to teach the following day. Not feeling too great, I skipped the drive to the airport, so I said goodbye to my mom as she and Sandy pulled away.

Despite the sadness of saying goodbye to my dad on Saturday and my mom that morning, I felt okay on Sunday as it was only day three of the chemotherapy cycle. I worked on my to-do list, which helped distract me from my fatigue and the gravity of my situation by forcing me to focus on the task at hand. After all, I had my final semester of college to worry about as the spring semester started on Monday.

My first class wasn't until Tuesday since I only had class on Tuesdays and Thursdays for the whole semester, so my final college semester technically began on Monday without any fanfare or class meetings. It was pretty anticlimactic. I made it to chapel on Monday, day four, and I heard a great message and caught up with friends after the holidays. That night, I crashed, knowing the ominous day five would greet me in the morning. The next day, I woke up slowly, took my medications, slept for another thirty minutes, and then took my time getting ready. I made it to my first Christian Thought class, a huge praise. I sat through class trying not to bolt out of there or make a scene with a surprise exit, and I thanked the Lord for keeping me in my seat for the full two hours of class. As I left, I texted my parents to let them know their tuition dollars were hard at work because I'd made it through class. So far, this day five wasn't as bad as my first two experiences. I went back to my house and, in keeping with my newest habit, I fell onto my bed, turned on my TV, and waited for the day to end.

IT'S OKAY TO BE IN PAIN

I dreaded days five and six. In the midst of my flu-like symptoms and feeling like my body attacked me, I wrestled with my inner thoughts, the purpose of those days, and the elusive idea of peace. Still, I figured I should make the best of my bad situation and put on a happy face. Most of the time, I wore my happy face well because I remembered I was doing okay in light of all the other terrible things that could happen. On days five and six, however, my happy face was buried too deeply under my pain and discomfort to fish out. I really struggled through those days, pleading and praying God would let me sleep and the day would pass quickly.

I love the book of Psalms, and I've found Warren W. Wiersbe's commentaries particularly helpful in my studies. In Psalm 6:6-7, David writes, "I am worn out from groaning; all night long I flood my bed with weeping and drench my couch with tears. My eyes grow weak with sorrow; they fail because of all my foes." Wiersbe writes of David and his simple plea for sleep:

> Whereas in the previous psalms, the Lord gave sleep and peace to David, here we find the king sleepless because of fear and pain. He was worn out from groaning, tossing, and turning, and he spent a good deal of time weeping. Sleeping had been replaced by suffering. Sleep is important for healing, so David's lack of sleep only made the condition worse... I've

learned that sickness and pain either make us better or bitter, and the difference is *faith*. If we turn to God, pray, remember His promises, and trust Him, we will find His grace sufficient for our needs. The Lord may not do what we ask, when we want it, but He will do what needs to be done and help us glorify His name. The question we should ask isn't, "When will I get out of this?" but, "What can I get out of this?"[3]

I identified with David because I'd spent my share of sleepless nights tossing and turning while pleading for peace. Instead of peace, it seemed my sleep had been replaced by more pain. However, I knew Wiersbe had a point. Amidst those sleepless nights and constant pain, I could choose to be bitter and look around at my decaying circumstances, or I could choose to get better and look upward, remembering God was sovereign, He knew my pain, He empathized with me, and He had a purpose in cancer.

My Aunt Sue followed my blog and read how I wanted the hardest days to pass quickly. I wrote that I was frustrated because there was little I could do to serve others on my worst days, but she left me an encouraging comment. She exhorted me to remember God has ordained every single day in our lives—yes, even the crappy ones when we feel so bad we pray for night to come. She encouraged me to trust that, even on my worst days when I didn't leave the house and couldn't physically serve the Lord, He still made each day useful. God knew I'd be feeling terrible time and again during chemo, and He had ordained those days, too. Rather than thinking I'd spent a day wasted by cancer, I could trust He had a purpose even in days five and six.

Her comment helped me greatly, and with each treatment, I reminded myself there was a reason for each day, praying God would use me despite my limited abilities. I'd prayed that many times before when I didn't feel adequate for the task He had for me, but it wasn't until I had cancer and was *physically* inadequate to do the job that I really grasped my limitations and prayed honestly.

In those days, I learned it was okay to be in pain. And more than *being* in pain, I learned it was okay for me to *admit* I was in pain. I've heard it said that people will admire your successes but identify with your struggles, and I saw that firsthand during cancer. Rather than always putting on my happiest facade, I learned to be real, acknowledge my pain, and go from there. I'm not endorsing self-pity or for us to lounge around wallowing in pain and bitterness. We could try that strategy, but I'm guessing we'll find it's not helpful and doesn't make the day any better. However, it's okay to admit we are in pain, we just need some sleep, and we are entirely dependent on the Lord.

A few chapters later, reflecting on Psalm 13, Wiersbe comments:

> We must not deny our feelings and pretend that everything is going well, and there is no sin in asking, "How long?" But at the same time, we must realize how deceptive our feelings are and that God is greater than our hearts (1 John 3:20) and can lift us above the emotional storms of life. David eventually learned to replace the question, "How long, O Lord?" with the affirmation, "My times are in Thy hands" (31:15). This is a lesson that all believers must learn.[4]

God is still greater than our cancer, our pain, our feelings, and our doubts, so it's okay to be honest about them.

CHOOSE JOY

As with many struggles in life, I found that with cancer, I had two choices: I could sulk about it, or I could fight it. Since it was inevitable that I would feel terrible, I decided I might as well make the best of things given the circumstances. Why would I want to feel doubly miserable because of the physical effects of cancer treatment added to the emotional baggage of sulking? People often remarked on my amazing strength, but I always told them two things. First of all, I was only hanging on by the grace and strength of the Lord. Secondly, the fact that I had cancer was inescapable, so I could choose to whine about it and be bitter, or I could choose not to let it overtake my life. I decided to embrace the catchphrase we'd used at Kanakuk that summer with my campers and "Choose joy."

In his book *Crazy Love*, Francis Chan writes about choosing joy. He explains,

> We tend to think of joy as something that ebbs and flows depending on life's circumstances. But we don't just lose joy, as though one day we have it and the next it's gone, oh darn. Joy is something that we have to choose and then work for. Like the ability to run for an hour, it doesn't come automatically. It needs cultivation. When life gets painful or doesn't go as we hoped, it's okay if a little of our joy seeps away. The Bible teaches that true joy is formed in the midst of the difficult seasons of life.[5]

What he says is true for so many reasons. True joy is formed and often made sweeter in the more difficult times in our lives. And it does ebb and flow, so it's unlikely we'll lose all joy or miraculously be full of it one day. But what I love most is his affirmation that it's okay if, in life's harder seasons, a little of our joy seeps away. It won't all disappear, but it's refreshing to know I'm normal when I'm not always singing joyfully amidst trying circumstances.

Think back to Christ's prayer in the Garden of Gethsemane: "'Abba, Father,' He said, 'everything is possible for You. Take this cup from me. Yet not what I will, but what You will'" (Mark 14:36). It's so freeing for me to know Christ wasn't looking forward to His imminent crucifixion, with the sin of the world on His shoulders and having the Father turn His face away. He prayed God would choose a different route to save the world. However, it is Christ's *ultimate* attitude of surrender that matters.

Amidst my trials, I've learned to say, "Not *my* will but *His* be done." It's okay if we're not thrilled nor looking forward to whatever trial we're in. It's okay if it frustrates us and is painful. It's even okay to let a little joy seep away and to cry out to the Lord that we don't like this. However, what really matters is turning that frustration, anger, and pain into submission, choosing to trust the Lord, and saying, "Not my will nor my way but *His* be done."

IT'S ALSO OKAY TO BE LIGHTHEARTED

While it's okay to admit we're in pain, it's also okay to enjoy the good days and have fun. Sometimes I think people didn't know what to make of my lightheartedness during cancer. It's not as if I always joked or spat out witty remarks; people who imagine cancer is a breeze from my happier days clearly missed all the days I spent holed up in my room, lights off and blinds closed, hoping the medicine would make me fall asleep so another day would end. I still shudder when I have vague reminders of how I felt on my worst days—it makes me nauseous and I don't like thinking about it. However, faced with doom and gloom all around, it was definitely a good idea to let off some steam and have fun when I felt like it. It's okay to joke about things—even cancer—and by continuing to laugh and keep my sense of humor, I think I let others breathe easier, too.

A tabletop cancer book I received was filled with tips on styling wigs, penciling on eyebrows, and keeping spirits high. The pages explain that fresh flowers have been proven to lighten cancer patients' days, bright colors are positive reinforcements, and lighthearted movies might be the only type of films patients want to see, and that's okay. I used to scorn chick flicks as being too cliché in their plots and unrealistic to life, but during cancer when stress pervaded my life, the last thing I wanted when I popped in a movie was something intense, heavy, or that kept me on the edge of my seat. I had enough of all that with my own real life saga. On the contrary, I wanted to see lighthearted movies, ones that didn't make me think but provided easy entertainment. Thus, in that year I saw more (previously avoided) chick flicks than I can count. And, I confess: post-cancer, I still appreciate those mindlessly cheerful movies for how they lightened my load and allowed me to check out. Cancer changed me in many ways...yes, even in my choice of entertainment.

After going through many unexpected situations, I've learned that we can't take ourselves too seriously. The ability to laugh at ourselves is crucial. While cancer is a serious diagnosis, there were times when all I could do was laugh and chalk things up to life being comical. In my first meeting with Dr. Gordon, he told me in very few cases, chemo can cause infertility. He explained some precautionary procedures I could seek such as taking birth control, harvesting eggs, and so on. When Dr. Gordon mentioned that doctors could preserve fertilized eggs of mine, my parents and I realized we are immature middle schoolers at heart. He said, "If there's anyone—a significant other—who you'd like to help you...fertilize your eggs.... You could think about that."

We barely held things together, and as soon as we left the oncologist's office, my dad joked, "Okay, which of your guy friends could we pay to 'fertilize your eggs'?" We erupted in laughter. While that may not strike you as hilarious, I'm convinced that appreciating the comedy, irony, and bizarre nature of life can definitely provide a respite from the tension of otherwise difficult situations. Keeping my sense of humor and shaking things off have been invaluable tools when going through trials, especially something with a tendency to rain on my parade like cancer. After my bizarre Christmas Eve chemotherapy treatment, all I could do was throw up my hands, admit that life is funny, and have a good laugh.

People always told me I had to stay positive, and I thought either, *How the heck am I supposed to stay positive? My body is attacking me!* or, *What exactly does that mean: "stay positive"?!? You try staying positive!* I finally figured out one of the best ways to stay positive was to make sure my friends and family members kept their senses of humor. My doctor was a huge advocate for continuing to live as normally as possible, and humor had always been a big part of my life, so I wasn't about to let cancer take my laughter away. Thankfully, my family also enjoys laughter, so it helped that they looked for humor in every situation.

Some of my favorite tension-relieving moments came from my younger sister Madelyn. When we first started talking about the potential for hair loss, she said three things that made us laugh. First she said, "Don't worry, Hannah, worst-case-scenario, you'll look like a naked mole rat!" That (apparently) was supposed to be comforting, she explained. Additionally, she said if I did lose my hair, I would look "pretty like a bald eagle and soar on the wings of Jesus." My family cracked up and told her we weren't aware Jesus had wings. Finally, after I had to shave my head, Madelyn saw me said, "You look like—in cartoons—when chickens get their feathers burnt off. But they're always so *cute* and everyone always loves the burnt, hairless chickens!" Insensitive? No. Just Madelyn trying to help lighten the mood and comfort her sister going through something otherwise grim and incomprehensible.

My dad's take on cancer treatment also helped alleviate the somber situation. When we were discussing radiation, he said, "You know, cooking you in the microwave is barbaric." After meeting with the oncologist for the first time and scheduling my first chemo, he added, "We had a good day yesterday, in spite of her being voluntarily poisoned." Both of these were delivered at precisely the right time, and though joking about cancer just seems wrong, it was an undeniable presence in my life, so ignoring it and treating it grimly wasn't helping anyone out and definitely didn't make it disappear.

Using humor also helped put others at ease so they didn't feel like they had to walk on eggshells around me. I mean, I was already being treated differently enough to begin with, so if others stopped having fun with me, my bad situation might only get worse.

My mom told me a co-worker of hers had cancer and went through the whole head shaving process one November. When it came time to take Christmas card pictures, it had been an obviously heavy year for them, so they wanted to have a lighthearted card. Someone got the idea to use her wig, so each of the kids and parents took individual pictures wearing her wig, and her oldest son Photoshopped them all together for a unique

Christmas card. If that isn't making lemonade out of lemons, then I don't know what is during cancer.

I remember my friend Liz Allbright first telling me about keeping a sense of humor when her mom faced death after months of failed treatment for pancreatic cancer. On a particularly bad day, Liz was in the car with her dad and brother, and Mrs. Allbright's worsened condition was the obvious elephant in the car, so to speak. Liz and her dad exchanged knowing glances, and then, from the back seat, her twelve year old brother Tyler piped up, "Well, it's not looking good for the home team," to which Liz and her dad erupted in laughter. I remember hearing that story in high school and wondering, *How can you joke about that?* but now I absolutely understand. Now I wonder how people *don't* joke when they're in such incomprehensible situations.

Would any of these comments or scenarios make it into a comedy routine? No. But were they hilarious in their time and crucial for somehow making sense of the gravity of cancer? Absolutely. If life hadn't already taught me to roll with the punches and let it happen, then cancer definitely would.

SETTING GOALS

On its website, the Mayo Clinic advises patients to set goals during treatment, and I found that advice helpful. I needed something to fight for and run toward during cancer. Finishing my college degree—and wrapping up the whole college experience, really—was a goal worth fighting for. Obviously, I was fighting to live, too, but I needed something to keep my mind off the constant barrage of cancer topics while providing me with a task to accomplish. It's great to check out from time to time and watch TV and movies. Trust me; I did more loafing around in those six months than I did in my first three years of college combined. However, working toward a goal is important in life and even more so when we have to keep our spirits up and need something to keep us engaged in the fight.

My goals were part of my situation in life, so I was fortunate. My mission in finishing college wasn't so much because I knew I needed to set goals, but it was more based on my desire to keep my mind busy, stay with my friends in our last semester together, and not miss out on the college experience. Coaching volleyball also helped me, and while I had to miss a few practices when the side effects from chemo overwhelmed me, I was still able to build relationships with kids, laugh at their fourteen-year-old antics, and have a blast with Brooke. I stayed connected to life, ministered to kids, and had fun.

Sometimes, the more time we have on our hands to sulk and ponder our ridiculous situations, the more our resolve to remain strong will be tested. To counteract that effect, I tried to stay engaged and distracted, setting some goals. I hoped to work out in the weeks right before chemo when I felt my best, but because it was so freezing during the main months of treatment and working out would have required me to either get a parking ticket or walk to the gym in the snow, my resolve for that goal slipped away pretty quickly. I shouldn't have let my goal fade so easily, but I also should have set reasonable goals, realizing cancer would slow me down in many ways. I couldn't do everything, and if I had tried, I probably would have ended up more exhausted and weak. At the same time, I did try to do *some* things. I didn't want to let cancer run my life or define me. Sure, it was a controlling factor, but it wasn't my *whole* life. The substance of who I was came down to so much more than cancer, before, during, and after it invaded.

STAYING ENGAGED

From the start, Dr. Gordon encouraged me to stay engaged in life as much as possible. I already wanted to remain engaged by staying at school, so I was—and am—so grateful for his stamp of approval on not letting cancer ruin my whole life. He told me I could go to chapel, classes, movies, parties, and other events, but he cautioned against attending concerts and sporting events in huge arenas with all kinds of germs. It's probably good neither he nor my nurses ever knew the extent of my travels and activities during cancer. I may not have been the *wisest* person by placing myself in germs' way, but I definitely enjoyed my senior year. In fact, having to fight against a constant drag on my system that tried to cramp my style made me both enjoy the things I could be involved in so much more and fight harder to have fun. That year I learned not to take my friends and the fun we had together for granted, and since I had to make a concerted effort to stay engaged, I appreciated everything I attended immensely.

Cancer didn't stop me from having a Newsies-themed movie night, though we had to have it at my house since it was -10 degrees and I couldn't go outside (which actually worked out well for me, given my aversion to the cold). Cancer didn't stop me from attending Wheaton's Senior Athletic Banquet, and though I threw up once in the bathroom during dinner and almost lost it while walking to the car afterward, I had a great time. Cancer didn't stop me from attending Wheaton's Senior Banquet, College Union's Roller Disco night, a trip to the Lyric Opera, and a Think Pink basketball game in which the school honored Kirsten and me while raising money and awareness for breast cancer.

Cancer didn't stop me from attending Wheaton men's basketball games—some of my favorite college events—despite the large crowds. Cancer didn't stop me from going to New York City with my Kanakuk co-counselor Melissa for spring break. Though I'm sure my doctors would cringe knowing I was in the most crowded and germ-ridden city in the US with a compromised immune system, I wasn't about to let cancer stop me from enjoying time with one of my best friends, my final spring break, and a city I love.

While I probably should have used more caution at times since my immune system bordered on empty, God protected me, and by His mercy (and energy), I was able to keep from checking out on life and still make so many great memories that year. Actually, my senior year of college, despite cancer, was my favorite year of college.

SEPARATING THE GOOD FROM THE BAD

When I got the news about my cancer, I learned many of my friends had seen their relatives and friends battle the disease. My friend Kristy shared about her dad's battle with cancer, and she helped me because she understood what I was going through. She told me her dad met with a psychiatrist during his treatment to help him process what was happening. Studies have shown those who maintain positive attitudes through cancer are more likely to beat the disease, so in one of his sessions, her dad had to literally visualize the chemotherapy in his mind as white knights battling off the evil dark knights, a.k.a. the cancer cells. The doctor told him to see the chemo as winning and defeating the evil cancer cells so as to engrain in his mind that, though the drugs made him feel terrible, they were actually the *good* team eliminating the diseased cells.

While Kristy and I laughed about the exercise, I understood its usefulness, and as an athlete, I resonated with the analogy. Sometimes it was hard to remember that cancer treatment was good. Many people say they felt like they had the flu, they had trouble exercising as they used to, or they had unexplained pain somewhere that led to their diagnoses. Since I had no symptoms (other than two swollen lymph nodes in my neck)—no fever, nausea, night sweats, or unexplained weight loss—before my diagnosis, the first time I ever felt poorly during my battle with cancer was after my first treatment of chemotherapy. It was really hard to accept chemo as the good guy when cancer itself had never affected how I felt. Truthfully, with every post-chemo check-up scan I've had, the thought has crossed my mind that if my cancer returned, part of me would want to just let it happen and skip the chemo. Yeah, that's crazy, but still...chemo sucks. I had to remind myself during each successive treatment, *This is good; it's saving my life; we* like *chemo*, to focus on the good.

I love music. I sing to myself most of the time—in my bedroom or car, while grocery shopping or grading papers, etc.—and songs often help me in times of struggle. I have countless playlists on my iPod from different events, for different seasons, regarding different emotions, and by different artists. When I was first diagnosed with cancer, my close friend Annie told me she'd heard a song on the radio that captured my situation, titled "Whatever You're Doing" by Sanctus Real. It begins, "It's time for healing," and goes on in the chorus to say, "Whatever You're doing inside of me, it feels like chaos, but somehow there's peace. And it's hard to surrender to what I can't see, but I'm giving in to something heavenly."[6] I think Sanctus Real intended the song to be a metaphor of God's spiritual healing in our lives, but that song spoke to my literal need for healing. I wasn't quite sure what God was doing inside of me, but whatever it was, I needed to surrender and trust that He was still in control.

I listened to the song and thought surely cancer merited its own playlist. I browsed my iTunes library and rounded up some great power jams for cancer, entitling the playlist "Hodgkin's Survivor Mix." It includes pop songs about survival and not giving up, worship songs about trusting in God's faithfulness, and a few solemn songs crying out for God to move, show what He's doing, and hold us. That playlist definitely helped me focus on the good and keep my spirits high, my heart engaged, and my will ready to fight.

I needed to separate the good from the bad, keep my eyes on the goal, and keep my spirit up however possible—whether by a playlist on my MP3 player, a steady display of flowers in my room, visualization techniques, or whatever else I had to do to remember that cancer might suck, but life was still worth living.

GOD = STRENGTH

On Memorial Day Sunday two years after chemo ended, I headed to One Love, my church in Honolulu, and noticed we had a guest speaker named Captain Gerald Coffee. I'll admit, sometimes I'm intrigued by guest preachers and at others I'm wondering why I didn't check up on that fact and sleep in. Shameful, I know. That Sunday I didn't know what to expect, but I left the service so touched by the speaker and how our very different situations actually bound us in certain ways that I determined never to doubt guest speakers again.

Captain Coffee began his story by telling us he'd been in the US Navy during the Vietnam War. While flying a combat mission over North Vietnam in February of 1966, his plane was shot down. Though he parachuted out, he was captured and spent the next seven years and nine days as a Prisoner of War in Hanoi.

He spent those seven years in a 6' x 3' jail cell. To put that in perspective, at a kennel I once called to see about boarding our dogs in the insufferable 100-plus degree Texas heat, the "Junior Suite" was 7' x 4'. For a dog. Okay.

Captain Coffee is a phenomenal speaker, and he wrote a book detailing his confinement, so I won't spoil all of it because it's definitely worth checking out. However, I would (with his permission) like to share a few of his ideas that so struck me with their parallels to cancer.

First of all, he talked about how faith in himself was crucial to his survival. His goal became to learn as much as he could within that time, recognizing and pursuing his duty as a soldier and believer. Accordingly, I think recognizing that, for whatever reason, God has allowed us to walk through difficult seasons should help us see our duty to rely on Him and learn as much as we can about Him and ourselves in the meantime.

Captain Coffee noted that keeping his sense of humor was key (sound familiar?). In addition, he said as a POW, he had to hack it out and be tough. He said he and his fellow prisoners "had to daily commit to do the things we do, simply because we could." For instance, the prisoners would pace back and forth—three steps and a turn—in their cells to keep their bodies in good physical condition. They were trained soldiers, so although they wouldn't fight outside of the prison for years, they kept up their shape as best as they could simply *because* they could. They walked miles in those cells by way of the three-step-and-turn route each day. This helped them have continued faith in themselves to bounce back and survive in order to return home in acceptable form.

Another point of his was how his faith in God to be his strength carried him through those years. Scratched on the wall of his cell were two words and a symbol: God = Strength. He said even just the seed of belief that with God, we can do anything, was enough to carry him. When he was stripped of all the things he used to identify with, he realized there is nothing other than God. When our world seems upside down and nothing is as we planned, we realize God is all we have and need.

My favorite song is "Closer" by Warren Barfield. It begins, "The sun should be halfway to China by now. The big lazy moon, well it's barely off of the ground. I'm on top of the world, but my world is upside down. And all I have is You. Come closer, closer than ever, so close to me. Come closer, closer than ever. When I have You, I have all I need."[7]

While I loved that song long before I went through cancer, I loved it even more during the battle. Though we may have nothing, we have the Lord, and He is more than enough to get us through each trial. Though my world felt upside down, God was not surprised and showed me He was more than enough to sustain me.

Captain Coffee and his fellow POWs relied on their training as soldiers to stay the course and on the Lord to be their daily strength. What I love most about Captain Coffee's speech is when he said, "There's nothing extraordinary about me. If I could survive that experience, so can you. We're all made out of the same clay."

When I first heard those words, I thought, *Okay, that's a nice, humble statement, but there's no way I could do that. Thanks for patronizing me, though.* But later, I realized I feel the exact same way about my experience with cancer. When people told my mom how well we were holding up or how they couldn't imagine going through something like that and doing so well, I loved her response. She said, "Two months ago, if you had told us we would be dealing with this, I would have said the same thing. You don't know how you'll get through it until you're in it and getting through it. You find that God meets you at every point of need." I'm no Xena-like warrior made with something unique. God didn't create me with some extra-special gene to look cancer in the face and laugh defiantly. If someone had told me ahead of time I would go through cancer, I probably would have laughed at him or her. And then I would have cried.

We *are*, actually, all made out of the same stuff. And we have a great and powerful God on whom we can rely. I think tales like Captain Coffee's inspire us but at the same time daunt us because we think we could never sit confined in a 6' x 3' cell for seven years (just writing that makes me need some air). Though his heroic struggle shouldn't be minimized—he's an amazing survivor with incredible willpower—if we were placed in his situation, God would also meet our needs.

The same truth applied to my cancer. It was okay to be afraid at times. It's *cancer*, for crying out loud! Let's be honest: if I was*n't* a little afraid, there was probably something wrong with me. The question for all of us amidst struggles is: Do we let our fear overtake and defeat us in our trials? Or, do we see that, though the way looks impossible to us, we have a God who is all-powerful and to whom nothing is impossible?

It isn't usually when we are in the midst of trials that God develops our character. On the contrary, in the middle of the storm, we kick into autopilot and fall back on the habits and character we've been building in the calmer seasons of life. That's why our daily habits, routines, and time with the Lord are so important. When life throws us curveballs, we don't have time to think about what to do; we simply deal with them as best we can. We use all the stores of faith, trust, and the knowledge of God we've cultivated when it's time to survive. God will be our strength and meet our needs when we walk through the fire, and there's a good chance we'll look back and wonder how we ever survived until we realize God carried us through every moment.

IT IS WELL

Sitting in chapel the day before my first chemotherapy treatment, I was a bundle of nerves. Singer Justin McRoberts played some of his music and then shared about himself. I love what he said when he sang the hymn, "It is Well." He explained how the lyrics have taken on a new meaning to him and said, "It is well with my soul, not because of the state of my pocketbook or circumstances, but because *my God* says it is well."

Whether my soul is well or not shouldn't be determined by my circumstances. We can't control our circumstances; we can, however, control our attitudes and how we *deal* with those circumstances. In chapel Justin explained, "Jesus Christ will never call you to a work that you *can* do on your own *without* Him; and He will never call you to something you *can't* do *with* Him. The goodness of God is better than the problems of the world."

If we can really embrace the last part—that, though this world can be a bummer, God is still better than those insurmountable problems—I think our attitudes will become more fearless. Justin's words helped me remember God hadn't called me to walk through cancer alone. God will never give us something so easy we can just breeze through it without leaning on Him. However, He'll also never give us something so difficult we can't get through it by relying on Him. He knows we can't do it alone. He also knows that with Him, we will always be able to answer His call.

I realized early on in my battle with cancer that my "fighting spirit" everyone kept praising me for was *not* going to cut it in beating my disease. My fighting spirit might help me, but it couldn't heal me. Only relying on the Lord to heal me was going to get me through this trial. Psalm 33:16-21 affirms this truth:

> No king is saved by the size of his army; no warrior escapes by his great strength. A horse is a vain hope for deliverance; despite all its great strength it cannot save. But the eyes of the Lord are on those who fear Him, on those whose hope is in His unfailing love, to deliver them from death and keep them alive in famine. We wait in hope for the Lord; He is our help and our shield. In Him our hearts rejoice, for we trust in His holy name.

No king, no matter how great and powerful his army, is saved by numbers or strength alone. The Lord *will* fight for us; we need only to be still (Exodus 14:14).

In his book *A Million Miles in A Thousand Years*, Donald Miller tells the story of Victor Frankl, a concentration camp survivor during World War II. Miller writes:

> Frankl's papers, written after surviving the camps, and even after losing his wife to the Nazis, indicated a philosophical conclusion that misery, though seemingly ridiculous, indicates life itself has the potential of meaning, and therefore pain itself must also have meaning.... Pain then, if one could have faith in something greater than himself, might be a path to experiencing a meaning beyond the false gratification of personal comfort.

> For the prisoners Frankl helped in the concentration camps, a chance for survival was increased by a person's ability to dwell in a spiritual domain, a place where the SS could not intrude. In essence, the prisoners whom Frankl influenced were convinced to surrender their tragic experiences to the greater whole of a grander epic, and in that role they found a purpose to continue living.[8]

Captain Coffee echoed Frankl's sentiment. He said everything changed for him when he stopped saying, "Why me?" and started saying, "Show me, God. Show me what I'm supposed to do with this." The title of his book is *Beyond Survival*, and his goal was to move beyond simply surviving the trial to emerge from it better than before.

What a great goal for us to embrace: that we wouldn't just scrape by but would learn to thrive, even when going through cancer; that we would remember no trouble—not the SS, not cancer, not death—can rob us of our relationship with Christ; and that there is a larger epic being told. If we can, as Frankl observed, surrender our pain and frustration to the fact that God is still in control and there's a whole lot more going on than we know or can imagine, I think we will find purpose in our struggle. We have to recognize there is a purpose to suffering and seek how God wants to use each trial. In doing so, we gain perspective and find the strength to press on while relying on Him to give us joy, keep our hearts light and spirits positive, heal our bodies, help us roll with the punches, and find meaning in the trial.

In the Word:

- **Psalm 28:6-7** "Praise be to the Lord for He has heard my cry for mercy. The Lord is my strength and my shield; my heart trusts in Him, and I am helped. My heart leaps for joy and I will give thanks to Him in song."

- **Psalm 31:9-10, 14-16** "Be merciful to me, O Lord, for I am in distress; my eyes grow weak with sorrow, my soul and my body with grief. My life is consumed by anguish and my years by groaning; my strength fails because of my affliction, and my bones grow weak.... But I trust in You, O Lord; I say, 'You are my God.' My times are in Your hands; deliver me from my enemies and from those who pursue me. Let Your face shine on Your servant; save me in Your unfailing love."

- **Psalm 73:25-26** "Whom have I in heaven but You? And earth has nothing I desire besides You. My flesh and my heart may fail, but God is the strength of my heart and my portion forever."

- **Proverbs 18:14** "A man's spirit sustains him in sickness, but a crushed spirit who can bear?"

- **Isaiah 40:29-31** "He gives strength to the weary and increases the power of the weak. Even youths grow tired and weary, and young men stumble and fall; but those who hope in the Lord will renew their strength. They will soar on wings like eagles; they will run and not grow weary, they will walk and not be faint."

- **Romans 15:13** "May the God of hope fill you with all joy and peace as you trust in Him, so that you may overflow with hope by the power of the Holy Spirit."

Other Resources:

- The book *What Cancer Cannot Do: Stories of Courage* (Grand Rapids: Zondervan, 2007) is a great pick-me-up and source of specific encouragement for those walking through cancer and their loved ones.

- For additional information on Captain Gerald "Jerry" Coffee check out his website (www.captaincoffee.com) or his book, *Beyond Survival: Building on the Hard Times—A POW's Inspiring Story* (Putnam, 1990).
- The Women Helping Others Foundation (www.whofoundation. org) has information and booklets for women with tips on setting goals, lifting spirits, seeking help, and feeling beautiful during cancer. Mail your request for a booklet to WHO Foundation, P.O. Box 816029, Dallas, TX 75381-6029 or fax a request to: 972-341-3080.

Arriving at the Robert H. Lurie Comprehensive Cancer
Center for my first appointment with Dr. Gordon

Playing in my final volleyball
match, knee-taped up and all,
three days before my casual trip to
Wheaton's health center. Photo ©
Michael Hudson Photography

Caroline and I try not to
laugh after my Christmas
Eve treatment in Dallas

The "before" picture from my head shaving
party with my Wheaton teammates

My hairdresser Melissa
Elledge trimming my hair
to lighten its weight

Harrison and I pose for "baldie"
pictures after I shaved his head

My best friend Melissa and me in
New York City during spring break

Brooke and me in our
coaching apparel at one of
our team's tournaments

My Wheaton teammates with me at a brunch my mom
threw to thank my friends for their help and love

The "Chemo Countdown" poster my mom's kindergarteners used to remember to pray for me and celebrate each treatment that passed

My nurse Michelle and I celebrate my final chemotherapy treatment

My family and me on my Wheaton College graduation day (from left: Brenda, Madelyn, me, Katie, Kevin)

CHAPTER 6

Hair Today, Gone Tomorrow

Wednesday, January 21, 2009

"The LORD is a refuge for the oppressed, a stronghold in times of trouble...for You, LORD, have never forsaken those who seek You" (Psalm 9:9-10).

Hello from Wheaton! Praise the Lord that the weather is warmer. And by warmer, I mean it's now in the positives. And hey! It looks like tomorrow's high is actually *above freezing*! I don't really know what to do with myself right now because I'm so thrilled (sad, isn't it?)!

I know so many have been praying, so I thought I should let you know that on Sunday night my volleyball teammates joined me as my teammate's mom shaved my head. So, if you've read the other posts, I am now officially "soaring on the wings of Jesus," in the words of Madelyn as she tried to comfort me about losing my hair. Actually, though, I was reading in Psalms last night and was at Psalm 17:8b which says, "Hide me in the shadow of Your wings," also a line from one of my favorite worship songs we sing at Wheaton called "Still." It turns out Madelyn's theology wasn't *too* far off; however, I'm pretty sure Psalm 17:8b is David's appeal for God to hide him in the shadow of His metaphorical wings rather than Madelyn's encouragement that I could soar on the literal wings of Jesus, but she tried at least.

God is so good in bringing peace. I think I've mentioned this, but over the events of the past year and a half, I've prayed a number of really specific times for God to give the "peace that passes all understanding," leaning hard on Philippians 4:6-7, and He has been faithful in providing. I prayed those words before the cutting/shaving began, and I know so many of you have been praying for peace, too. The night was such a testimony to God's faithfulness and following through on the things He promises. He truly and mercifully gives a peace that makes me think, *How in the* world *am I so calm right now?* and I know it's only because the Lord is at work.

Once again, thank you. I am so touched. Plus I'm becoming so much less cynical and fiercely self-reliant as I trust others and allow people to help me. Your encouragement continues to floor me again and again. Know that you are being faithful to God's call to carry one another's burdens and encourage one another in love. You have blessed me so much!

On Christ the solid Rock I stand,

Hannah
Posted at 10:05 p.m.

THE ELEPHANT IN THE ROOM

Now we come to the thing no one wants to talk about: hair loss. Time and again, this is one of the most recognizable side effects of cancer. You see a bald girl? She probably has cancer, you assume, and rightly so. Let's be honest: hair is normal; baldness isn't. This truth even applies to men. Think about how many men go to great lengths to preserve their hair at the first signs of balding or grayness (e.g. comb-overs, Rogaine, midlife-crisis-inspired hair dye, etc.). A recent ABC News report estimates that men spend over $1 billion annually to combat baldness,[9] so if it's a big deal for the average man, baldness is understandably a big deal for someone already dealing with cancer.

My sister Katie works at a children's hospital in Florida, and she and her co-workers are always dumbfounded at patients' fear of losing their hair. She had one patient recently diagnosed with terminal cancer, but despite the news, all the patient could think about was losing her hair. Katie said she and her co-workers think people worry so much about hair because it's a very visible sign of the disease waging war internally. To some onlookers, on a bad day of nausea and other side effects, a cancer patient might just seem really sick, but when others see that shining scalp, the "C word" is all too identifiable. Whether it's the outward sign people can't come to grips with or not, all I could think about was how bald people reminded me of the Conehead mask my dad used to wear to scare my sisters and me when we were young.

As soon as I heard my diagnosis, I thought, *Please, not my hair!* Now, I don't consider myself overly vain, and we're all a little insecure, but I do remember telling my parents that the thing I liked best about me was my hair. My mom's best friend Sandy told me about her friend who had scores of people praying she wouldn't lose her hair, and she didn't. With her chemo regimen, it was almost certain she would, so keeping her hair was a huge answer to prayer. After hearing her story, I decided to rally my prayer team, asking for specific prayers that I wouldn't lose my hair even though research said I probably would. I figured what a cool testimony to God's miraculous power it would be if I kept my hair. In my mind, I envisioned my nurses and doctors being dumbfounded as I showed them my hair and said, "It's all because of the Lord!" I thought, *Wouldn't that be a great opportunity to witness, God?* That's where projecting our plans onto the Lord can get us into trouble. Sure, God could've done that, but He chose a different way.

I think people hope that, by ignoring this topic, nothing will change, but once I finally did start asking people—from my hairdresser to my doctors to those who'd traversed this road before me—I heard a lot of different advice. Many people even offered their unsolicited opinions on how I should proceed. Some people told me to shave my hair off right away to save myself from the traumatic experience of losing it. Or recall what the doctor I saw on Christmas Eve told me: "You know, your scalp's gonna itch and burn and then *wham*! All your hair's just gonna fall out." Luckily, things didn't happen quite that way.

Some of the more sensitive doctors said because I had thick hair, I might only lose some of it. Since my hair fell to the middle of my back, the hospital staff said its weight might cause more hair to fall out than if it was shorter. They advised me to preventatively cut it shorter just in case.

When I was home for Thanksgiving after my biopsy but before I got my diagnosis, I went to my hairdresser Melissa Elledge to get a trim. I'd been going to her for haircuts since I was in seventh grade, so we'd known each other for a long time. Tears filled her eyes when I told her cancer was a possibility, and she said if the diagnosis was positive, she would help me with my hair. It turns out she used to volunteer with the American Cancer Society during college, styling wigs, cutting hair, and helping patients apply makeup and draw on eyebrows.

Research said my hair would start to fall out around two weeks after my first chemo treatment, so one day over Christmas break, my mom and I met Melissa at her house. She cut thirteen inches off my hair into two ponytails (I wasn't kidding when I said it was thick). I donated both of the ponytails to Locks of Love, figuring my hair should at least help *someone*. I tried to embrace my short locks, hoping things wouldn't get worse and that I wouldn't be on the receiving end of donated hair anytime soon.

In the meantime, remembering all of the advice and knowing full well the Rascal Flatts song "Skin," which talks about a girl waking up and finding hair on her pillow, I fell asleep each night dreading what I might find when I awoke. With a one-eyed, half grimacing glance where I didn't want to look but knew I had to, I'd check out my pillow. Christmas day fell exactly two weeks after my first chemo treatment, so imagine my anxiety followed by great relief when I checked my pillow that morning to see only the orange pillowcase.

Day by day passed, and three weeks after my first treatment, my hair still survived. When people warned me about losing my hair, they always mentioned it coming out in "clumps." I figured that meant I'd grab a chunk of hair and pull it right off of my head—like Velcro or something— leaving an awkward bald patch. That never happened. Instead, when I brushed it, more and more strands came out than before. I thought I was out of the woods once I made it past week four, but I was wrong. Heading into the middle of the fifth week after my first treatment, I finally came to terms with reality.

The process of how I decided to shave my head was important. After the new year began, every time I washed my hair, I lost more and more of my remaining strands. A week and a half into my spring semester at Wheaton, I reached a point where I didn't want to wash my hair because I knew I'd lose more, and I felt like it was barely hanging on as it was. The only problem was, as you can imagine, my hair started looking nastier with each passing, unwashed day. Thus, I didn't want to leave my house. It was a cyclical problem because I wouldn't wash my hair so that it wouldn't fall out, but then my hair looked dirty and stringy, so I didn't want to be seen with it, and on and on it went. Finally, I knew it was time to say goodbye.

I needed to get to that point—where I was no longer afraid of saying goodbye to my hair because I was so appalled by it—and I think people going through this need to get to that point as well. Of all the advice I received, my mom's helped the most: shave it only when ready. All the people with the opinions on hair loss were well-meaning, but realistically, most of them hadn't shaved their heads. I was so torn about what to do that it was relieving when my mom said, "You know what? None of us has ever been there before, and though we can try to imagine what it feels like, we can't really understand what you have to do, so you get to do what *you* want to do. You can shave it now, or you can hold on to it until there's one strand on your scalp, and we won't blame you. It's *your* hair, and you can do whatever you want with it, baby." Only a mom can understand and reassure like that. Her advice took so much pressure off of me. I realized there was no "right" way to approach my hair dilemma, so when my attachment to my locks turned to disgust at their dirty, stringy condition, I was ready to say goodbye. And once I was ready, shaving my head turned out to be way easier than if I'd still felt some lingering attachment to my straggling, Phantom of the Opera-like hair.

THE BIG EVENT

Knowing what I had to do, I texted Kaitlyn, one of my freshmen teammates. Her family lived in Wheaton, and early on in my diagnosis, they offered to assist me in any way possible. Her mom Robin is a hairdresser who said she'd be more than happy to help me out if I had to shave my head. Still hoping my hair might hold on, I hadn't wanted to commit to anything at the time, but in January when I had to wear a beanie just to leave the house, I decided to pull the plug. Brooke and I had a volleyball tournament that day, so we talked about the decision, and she said she'd be there to help me. I figured Kaitlyn should be there since her mom would be hosting, and with a couple of my teammates there already, I went ahead and invited the rest of them over, too. Initially, I didn't want anyone there. I mean, knowing I would be bald was weird enough, and I'd heard that shaving my head might be semi-traumatic. However, once two friends were coming, I bit the bullet, swallowed my pride and vanity, and texted the rest of my teammates, asking them to come over. And I'm incredibly thankful I did.

Some of their responses read,

"I'll be there. Hannah, we love you so much,"

"I for sure want to be there. Let me know more when you can," and,

"Oh Hannah...I'm there all the way."

In addition to being glad I made the hair decision when I was ready, I'm also glad I didn't traverse that road alone. As embarrassing and awkward as shaving a head can be, having people there to support me made the awkward night so much easier and actually turned something I dreaded into a really great memory.

On Sunday, January 18th, my teammates caravanned to Kaitlyn's house for the big event. Obviously I dreaded what would happen, but some of my teammates were wide eyed and scared, too. Thankfully, everyone put on their bravest fronts to support me. First, we ate dinner and caught up on life. Robin turned on praise music, and as dinner ended, the time arrived to say goodbye to my hair. She gathered everyone around me and took a "before" picture. Then everyone laid hands on me and Robin prayed for me. Her sweetness and encouragement made the whole night incredibly easy. Before she shaved my head, Robin had a fun idea that each of my teammates would cut off some of my locks first, so with my approval, each teammate came up and trimmed my hair. That definitely took some trust on my part and skill on theirs, and once they finished and my chin length locks were gone, Robin used a razor to buzz my hair. It was the strangest feeling—like a massage on my scalp—and all of a sudden, my scalp was free and chilly and my head felt lighter. She took me over to the kitchen sink to rinse off my scalp, and afterward I sat back down in the chair. Then Robin said she wanted to pray again.

In all of the discussions about my hair, though I'd been nervous, I never cried because ultimately I knew some things were inevitable no matter how much I lamented them. However, as Robin prayed for me, I started crying, but not in mourning over my fallen tresses. During the prayer, my teammates gathered around me, holding me and letting me know they were with me. Some were crying, and I was touched by their encouragement and love. To think that they were crying over me was humbling, and I was overwhelmed with how God so perfectly provides support. Their tears reminded me that this journey was much bigger than just *my* battle with cancer. If someone had told me earlier I would cry at my head shaving, I would have figured it would be over the trauma of being bald. However, there I was crying because I was overwhelmed with love and joy.

The Lord turns our darkness into light—yes, even when our darkness is a shallow and vain topic like hair. God turned my sorrow into joy. I've mentioned that I often pray Philippians 4:6-7, for the peace that passes all understanding, and God has consistently overwhelmed me with an unaccountable calm and serenity amidst many stressful situations. So many times I've wondered, *How am I so calm right now?* only to conclude it's because God is at work, not because of some inner fortitude.

At a class retreat with the school where I teach, I shared about that night with my students, choking up as I recounted it. I'm really not an emotional person (though this book might make it sound otherwise). In any average, non-cancer year I cry maybe twice, but I get choked up often when I remember how good the people of God were throughout cancer. Most of my teammates had plans that night. Some were going out to dinner, others had Bible study, and a couple had dates with their boyfriends, but all of them cancelled whatever they had going on to support me. As a cynic who thinks people will inevitably fail me, I was humbled by the importance of community and fellowship. Had I taken a trip to my hairdresser alone as originally planned, I probably would have thrown a pity party for one, mourning my lost locks and drowning in misplaced sorrow. Instead, by swallowing my vanity and pride to let others join me, I ended up blessed.

Before we left Kaitlyn's house that night and returned to campus, we went into the bathroom and the girls made me model my wigs. One teammate timidly asked if she could try one on, and when I agreed, each of my teammates followed suit. It was hilarious and a great note on which to end the night. I saw my brunette teammates go blonde, curly haired friends check out straight hair, girls with short hair try out longer locks, and teammates without bangs experiment with new possibilities. After the fun ended, we headed back to campus and I stopped at my teammates Stef and Kelli's place. They sat with me for a while as we talked and they helped me process what had just happened. One of their roommates asked what we'd been up to, and she was shocked to hear Robin had just shaved my head. She said the wig looked very realistic and her comment reassured me that, for the most part, the wig brought some normalcy.

Soon I went back to my house and pulled out the Hawaiian print satin pillowcase my grandma had sewn and sent me in the mail. I'd heard sleeping on a satin or silk pillowcase felt better than cotton on a shorn scalp, and as I settled into bed, emotionally and physically beat, I nodded off thinking about how smooth and strange my scalp felt on my pillow.

TO WEAR A WIG OR NOT?

Before my path and Kirsten's intertwined, I remembered seeing a girl around campus who always wore a baseball cap over her bald head. College kids tend to make statements with their clothing and choices, so I wasn't sure if she was trying to rock the bald look or if she had cancer. When I heard prayer requests for Kirsten in chapel and started undergoing all of my tests, I realized she was probably the girl we prayed for.

Prior to my head shaving, I worried about whether to wear a wig or not. Other questions followed such as if a wig would be tax-exempt, if I should get a synthetic or human hair wig, and what color, style, and look to choose. Kirsten's bravery in facing baldness head-on, throwing on a baseball cap, and not worrying about what others thought impressed me. I'd like to say I didn't care at all what people thought and embraced the look. However, at the time, I cared a little bit. But maybe more than caring what people thought about my baldness, I was daunted at the thought of just putting it all out there and visibly reminding people—and myself—I was "that cancer girl."

One night as Brooke and I drove to volleyball practice, we discussed my dilemma. I told her I felt bad because I didn't *want* to care about others' opinions. I wanted to be so brave that I went around bald—it would sure save time, money, and effort. At first I wondered if God was testing me and trying to humble me. Maybe I was supposed to walk around bald as a sign of obedience. Then I realized I was over-thinking the implications of hair loss.

I didn't want to walk around bald, but I hated most that I was so vain to even make this an issue. I felt guilty because I knew things like appearance weren't supposed to matter to believers. Brooke then told me about her best friend's mom, Beverly, who battled cancer and lost her hair. Brooke greatly admires Beverly for her confidence and carefree spirit. However, she wore a wig every single day of her journey through cancer. Brooke never saw her without the wig, and though Beverly is a godly woman who doesn't worry about what others think, she decided she was happier wearing a wig. When people told her how much they loved her hair (not knowing it was a wig), she responded by saying, "It's not even real!" or, "Do you want it, too? I can let you wear it!"

For some reason, though I'd never met this woman, Beverly's story was freeing and I appreciated Brooke passing it on. If a fifty year old wife and mother—who was supposed to have things figured out—felt better with a wig, then somehow it wasn't vain, immature, or wrong for me to wear one either. I recalled my mom's words: I get to do what I want.

Ultimately, it's about what the person actually faced with the decision wants to do. If people want to wear a wig every second of the day (even while sleeping), they should go for it. It's their choice, and they're neither wrong nor vain to want some normalcy. If others think wearing a wig sounds itchy and too high-maintenance, then they don't have to wear one. Either way, the decision is a good one when they're comfortable with it. Now, that principle isn't universal; it's not as if God says, "Hey, sure, go run wild and crazy. No worries, man. Whatever you're comfortable with must be good!" But I tend to think during cancer, it's okay to make some decisions for ourselves, especially regarding hair. I don't think God was disappointed with me for choosing to wear a wig.

I still learned not to worry about what people thought. Since I'd gone from short, thinning hair to the wig's long, thick hair in one day and most people knew I had cancer, it wasn't too hard for them to put two and two together and realize I was bald underneath my wig. I was humbled and stripped of vanity by virtue of shaving my hair in the first place. More than any other benefit, the wig was a way for me to avoid always standing out like a sore thumb. Cancer overall has taught me to not care what people think because so much is out of my control, but even now if I had to go back through the process, I'd pull out my old wigs and wear them all the time. Since having cancer made me stand out to begin with, I wanted to feel as normal and beautiful as I could despite my circumstances, and I think that's okay.

I felt relieved to know I wasn't selfish, a failure, or the most vain person on the planet if I wore a wig or cared that my hair was falling out. It's normal to have hair, and even to the most self-assured people, hair loss is still a strange and unsettling process. Now, if that became my preoccupation and I spent hours each day trying to look presentable, I would have had an issue—not only of pride and vanity, but also of time and energy. When feeling terrible, spending hours primping in front of the mirror is a pretty bad undertaking. I learned that sometimes, it's just better to call a spade a spade, throw on a wig, and say, "This is as good as it's gonna get," given the reality of the situation.

WIGGING OUT

Over Christmas break while I was home with my family, my parents wanted to prepare for the worst, so they dragged me reluctantly to a wig store. I tried on multiple styles of wigs—some with long hair, others with short; monofilament wigs with a transparent base allowing the natural scalp to peek through; wigs of various shades; and human hair and synthetic wigs. In keeping with my "fly below the radar" mentality, I decided to go with something pretty close to my natural hair color and thickness. I wasn't up to going with a whole new look and eliciting even more attention than I already received because of cancer. I started off with one synthetic wig and one real hair wig. I took them with me in their shoeboxes back to college and put them on a high shelf in my closet, hoping I'd never have to see them again but thankful I had them when mid-January rolled around. My wigs came in boxes with tags advertising their styles and colors, so I ended up naming each of my wigs based on their tags, referring to them affectionately as Aspen, Honey, Spring, and Brittany.

I learned a few things about wigs. First of all, synthetic wigs are much cheaper than human hair wigs, and for good reason. They're basically made of plastic—think Barbie hair—so they get tangled and start to show wear after a month or two. Also, since they're made of plastic, if I stood too close to a heat source like an oven or a campfire, my wig could burn or melt. After wearing my synthetic wigs for around three months, it was time to retire one and move on to the next model because they started to look like Felicity, my American Girl doll, whose hair was so ratty I had to send her in for a "head transplant" when I was younger. Though synthetic wigs are cheaper, when I wore them all the time, I ended up buying multiple wigs for the duration of treatment, which added up.

My human hair wig was expensive. Though we were told some insurance companies covered wigs with a doctor's note under "cranial prosthesis," our policy didn't. Thankfully my parents were willing to buy me one. The wig arrived and was beautiful but very thick, and it looked heavy. I liked my human hair wig because I could straighten, curl, and blow dry it—pretty much anything I could do to normal human hair worked. However, I quickly learned that human hair wigs have their drawbacks.

Just like hair on our scalps, real hair wigs react to things like snow, rain, and other weather adversely. I was surprised to see the wig's hair was curly the first time it got wet. It's amazing how companies assemble the wigs because each one is made up of around three to six ponytails. To get a similar texture, length, and style from three different people is a feat. My hairdresser Melissa saw my wig and agreed it looked too heavy, so she promised to fix it and took it home with her for a week. When I met back up with her, I saw a beautiful wig. She had thinned and highlighted it for free, and conveniently, no roots would ever show in this hair.

On days when I woke up with little time to get ready, I threw on a synthetic wig, but on days when I had time to work with the hair or wanted to curl it for a nice event, I wore the human hair wig. I never left my house without a wig on, and I was okay with that, remembering the decision to wear a wig or not was mine alone. It was my hair (or lack thereof), and those around me were probably very well-meaning with their advice, but they weren't in my shoes.

SOLIDARITY

Back in November when I began undergoing tests and knew I needed a biopsy, I had breakfast with a couple of my closest friends, Lisa and Harrison. Not knowing then that I had cancer, but fully aware the word "biopsy" conjures such a possibility, I was a little tense. As Lisa proceeded carefully in asking what was up, Harrison bluntly told me, "Alright. If you get cancer and lose your hair, I'll let you shave my head." Lisa hit him on the shoulder, telling him something along the lines of no girl ever wanting to think about that, especially when I might or might not even have cancer. I laughed it off and said it was fine and that I'd hold him to his word, but later when I sat down to think about his comment, I knew hair loss was something I feared. Many people hear "cancer" and associate the word with bald heads and pasty skin, and since those effects happen to many patients, they're not bad assumptions. However, that's probably not how a cancer patient wants to be thought of.

A few months after that meal, I was working through my to-do list and called Harrison. I'd been meaning to catch up with him, but I also remembered his promise. I wasn't really going to make him shave his head, but I wanted to mess with him and see if he would try and go back on his word. I said, "Well, I don't know if you remember, but a couple of months ago, you made a little deal with me." He asked me to jog his memory, so I told him I'd shaved my head the night before. Harrison said, "Okay, do you want to come over in an hour?" Surprised, I said, "Wait, are you serious? You don't actually have to do this," but he insisted.

An hour later, I walked to Harrison's house and he met me with his electric razor and towel ready to go. I was nervous about shaving his hair too closely, but he reassured me I was fine, showing me the safety on the blade that wouldn't let me scalp him, so I went ahead and buzzed his hair. One of his roommates came downstairs to admire the work and then said we needed a picture together. I took off my wig and we took some baldy pictures together. I hugged Harrison and thanked him repeatedly.

That night at the men's basketball game, I saw Harrison again, and everyone commented on his newly shaved hair. I smiled thinking he'd let me do that. It didn't make my baldness go away, and he would tell you (as he's reminded me many times) it was no big deal for him as a guy, but it was one way a friend helped ease the discomfort and toll cancer took on my life. And, though his hair slowly grew back while mine was still M.I.A., I appreciated having someone in solidarity with me even for a short time.

UNEXPECTED ENCOURAGEMENT

Time passed, and wearing my wigs became strangely routine. In mid-April, a few months after my head shaving party, I received a letter in the mail from someone in Missouri. Having no idea who sent it, I opened it, curious to find out. Inside was a double-sided note card, and flipping to the back page, I saw that it was from Meredith, one of my former Kanakuk campers. She won an all-camp award for serving others and loving people selflessly, and I learned more from her that summer than I ever could have taught her. In a relationship where I was the counselor and should have been writing my camper letters, Meredith picked up my slack and encouraged me instead.

Since she has a genuine spirit and kind heart, I figured the note contained her condolences and prayers, but as I started to read, I was surprised. She did tell me how she loved, missed, and was praying for me, but then she moved on to explain how I had helped her understand that God has a great plan despite our doubts. As if I wasn't touched enough by her thanking me, Meredith went on to say,

> I also want to share with you something else that's going on in my life! This Friday at 4:30 p.m. (you may not have needed to know the time...but now you do! Well back to the point), I have decided to cut off my hair for Locks of Love. Hair, I believe, is one thing girls really do take for granted, besides being in a situation like yours. Reading and seeing in your blog about cutting your hair really cut right through me. I know this is a silly and maybe even childish realization. But, for me, hearing you tell about cutting your hair stopped me dead with understanding how extremely serious all of this is.

> With all that said, it has made me come to the decision to cut my hair so that some girl or boy will be able to have it. I know it's not much but is something I can help with—knowing that someone else will be able to have some beautiful hair!

> I want you to know that I pray for you constantly—at every meal, throughout the day, FCA, youth group, and sticky notes of every treatment on my mirror! LOL. Through everything I know God has blessed you and will continue doing so.

> I love you! Meredith

Now, aside from my gratitude for her fervent prayers and thoughts of me—I mean, what a sweet sixteen year old!—I was floored. While Robin shaved my head, I definitely wasn't thinking that God might use this to do big things in other people, too. I was encouraged that, even in this trial, God was working in and through me somehow. Not only was He teaching Meredith, but He was also using her lessons to bless other cancer patients in the future. I was humbled by the fact that this whole experience, including my hair loss, was bigger than me. God was using the experience of cancer in my life to teach and grow me in incredible ways, but He also taught and grew countless others through different steps of the journey.

NO BIG DEAL

I love surfing. Whether I'm watching it or standing on my board riding the waves as if I'm walking on water, it's awesome. Living in Hawaii after college has given me some good opportunities to watch surfing events, and one Thursday in November when Sarah, one of my closest friends, was in town, we went up to the North Shore of Oahu. One of the legs of the Vans Triple Crown of Surfing was slated to start the following day, so we went to be near the action. I didn't anticipate seeing professional surfer Bethany Hamilton.

After Bethany lost her arm in a shark attack in 2003, I remember reading her book *Soul Surfer* the following summer at camp. It was a great book, and I've always been inspired by her story. As Bethany came on shore, I briefly said hello, it was nice to meet her, and how grateful I was for her incredible faith and bold testimony. She was appreciative, but I didn't want to annoy her during a practice session, so I waved goodbye and walked back to my towel. It was a cool moment. I haven't met too many celebs, and I probably wouldn't just go up and talk with many if I did, but I felt like thanking Bethany for telling her story.

When I saw the movie based on her story, I remembered her incredible bravery, strength, and faith amidst a crazy situation. What's most amazing to me is how she doesn't feel like a brave heroine. On the contrary, she talks about how she could either sink or swim, and she chose to stay afloat and do the things she could and was called to do. Furthermore, friends comment that she's "totally over" her arm being gone. It's hard for me to imagine that having one arm could ever become the new normal, but in perspective, Bethany says it simply isn't a big deal. She's grateful that she's alive, she can still surf, and this otherwise tragic accident has given her a great platform for sharing her faith around the world.

Her story helped put my problems in perspective. Though my hair might come back a different color or texture after treatment—it came back slightly darker and very curly—it should eventually return to normal. Though it seemed like my hair took forever to grow back, others were impressed by the speed with which it reappeared. Though I felt like a Conehead without hair or a wig, others thought I had a beautiful and nicely shaped head (yep, I was told many times that my head was very nicely shaped). Though I felt vain and embarrassed at times, others called me brave and admirable for having lost my hair. Though I felt like an imposter with a wig, others usually didn't notice. And, though at times losing my hair felt like an enormously big deal, fighting to stay alive was unquestionably the more important issue.

If I needed to mourn the loss of my hair, that was okay...for a little while. It was okay to lament the changes and side effects wrought by cancer on my body. But, at the same time, I had to remember I was so much more than my hair. I was so much more than anything the side effects of cancer treatment could do to me. And ultimately, I was so much more than cancer.

Bethany's story reminded me that if she, and so many others like her, can survive the permanent loss of a limb and call it "no big deal," then I'm pretty sure I can handle my temporary hair loss. Sometimes we need a dose of reality to see the bigger picture and realize all is not lost even when our hair or health is.

FEARFULLY AND WONDERFULLY MADE

As camp counselors to insecure middle school girls for three summers during college, my co-workers and I always tried to help our kids remember they were beautiful and God had made them just as He wanted. We often quoted Psalm 139:14, "I praise You because I am fearfully and wonderfully made; Your works are wonderful, I know that full well," to encourage our campers and remind them God had created them purposefully. I've always known that verse, and while it seemed like a helpful catchphrase for encouraging my campers, the truth of the psalm finally hit home when I was bald.

When I had hair, even on bad hair days or when my face broke out, I reminded myself that God had created me with great intention and care. On those days, I knew underneath my then-scruffy appearance that I had potential and things could get better, and my unsightly days were made better with such knowledge. However, one day shortly after we shaved my head, I looked in the mirror and saw a couple of loathsome moles on my head along with my shorn scalp, and that verse came to mind. I was frustrated with the reality of my situation: my bald head, purple-tinted chemo skin, sunken eyes, and a lack of eyebrows. God clearly knew I needed encouragement. The verse reminds us God is sovereign, above all things and over all things, having created everything exactly to His purpose and plan. He created me fearfully and wonderfully—yes, even with my tufty hair and sickly countenance. I stood there and repeated His truth to myself over and over: "I am fearfully and wonderfully made."

My appearance did not change the fact that God had crafted me exactly to His purpose, and I was still His precious and beautiful daughter even though I sure didn't feel or look that way at the time. It was hard to truly embrace that truth, but I kept re-reading the verse and reminding myself that, even then, God had not made a mistake. The status of my hair didn't change the fact that I was fearfully and wonderfully made, and not only physically, but in who I am, beyond what my reputation and looks are to my character, my dreams, my strengths, and even my weaknesses. In short, as Kanakuk's president Joe White always says, "God don't make junk," not even when I clearly looked like cancer had the upper hand. But because God doesn't make junk and I could remember I was just as fearfully and wonderfully made as the day I was born, cancer wouldn't have the upper hand.

In the Word:

- **Isaiah 46:4** "Even to your old age and gray hairs I am He, I am He who will sustain you. I have made you and I will carry you; I will sustain you and I will rescue you."
- **Matthew 10:29-31** "Are not two sparrows sold for a penny? Yet not one of them will fall to the ground apart from the will of your Father. And even the very hairs of your head are all numbered. So don't be afraid; you are worth more than many sparrows."
- **1 Peter 3:3-4** "Your beauty should not come from outward adornment, such as braided hair and the wearing of gold jewelry and fine clothes. Instead, it should be that of your inner self, the unfading beauty of a gentle and quiet spirit, which is of great worth in God's sight."

On the Web:

- Pantene Pro-V's Beautiful Lengths program partners with the American Cancer Society to give wigs to women with cancer. Check out how to donate at www.pantene.com and head to the Beautiful Lengths tab, or to check on receiving a wig, call the ACS Wig Bank line at 1-877-227-1596.
- The American Cancer Society's partner site, Tender Loving Care (www.tlcdirect.org) offers products for hair loss from wigs and scarves to wig stands and eyebrow stencils.
- Head Huggers (www.headhuggers.org) makes knit hats for patients suffering hair loss. Check out the website for more info, to receive a hat, or for guidelines on how to make and submit a hat for someone. Heavenly Hats (www.heavenlyhats.com) provides caps and hats free of charge to patients with hair loss.

CHAPTER 7

God Is Sovereign

Monday, March 2, 2009

"Your love, O LORD, reaches to the heavens, Your faithfulness to the skies. Your righteousness is like the mighty mountains..." (Psalm 36:5-6a).

What a great Psalm! I'm sure many of you know this from the worship song aptly titled "Your Love O Lord." I vividly remember standing on a beach in the Dominican Republic the summer after my senior year of high school singing this song. It was the end of an incredible and life-changing mission trip with my youth group from Bent Tree Bible Fellowship, and our team of eleven students and two leaders was debriefing at a hotel in Santo Domingo. Part of that debriefing included worship time on our last night, and that's where we come to me, standing on the beach, facing the ocean, with mountains in the distance, a full moon, and not a cloud in the sky, singing this song and understanding it in such a real way. That was probably the second greatest night of my life. Looking out to my surroundings, I got such an incredible visual of these words: "Your love O Lord, reaches to the heavens. Your faithfulness stretches to the sky. Your righteousness is like the mighty mountains. Your justice flows like the ocean's tide." The song goes on to say, "I

133

will lift my voice to worship You my King. I will find my strength in the shadow of Your wings."[10]

I've always loved these words and that great visual image, and they are such a good reminder in a time like this. On our trip, basically our whole construction plans of pouring a foundation for a building at an orphanage were thwarted by an approaching hurricane that drenched the site and flooded the trenches for our foundation. Instead of accomplishing a good amount of manual labor, we ended up trying to get water (and nasty frog eggs) out of the trenches each day, fixing rebar, and wondering dejectedly why we were the most underachieving team our church had ever sent to the DR. However, since our elaborate construction plans changed, the missionaries came up with "plan B," which was to help clean one of the houses on site that our team the year before (which I was a part of) had built, readying it for the first orphans to inhabit. Long-story-short, unexpectedly, we got to move the first people into the mission site, the fulfillment of the missionary's dream and the culmination of twenty-five years of work to accomplish that dream.

The whole experience typified what I've learned many times since. Often (and especially in my life), life strays from "the plan," which can often seem like failure. The night we moved those orphans into their new home was one of the greatest nights of my life, and we wouldn't have been able to do that had the rain not thwarted our original plans. That lesson rings true today. Hey, I never would have picked lymphoma to cap off my senior year of college, and like bailing out frog infested waters in trenches in the DR, God's plan is not always fun or easy, but His promises are true, and the end is always better than we can imagine.

The night after the orphans settled in was the one on the beach, and that night, everything was so clear and put into great perspective. His love truly never ends. His faithfulness is beyond the heights up in that clear expanse of never-ending blue. His righteousness is high and bold like those mountains in the distance. His justice is as deep as that ocean and keeps on coming like the tide. Today, I need that reminder. Out of every situation in my life, my response should be to lift my hands and voice to worship my King, as well as to truly find my strength in the shadow and comfort of God alone. I'll be honest: some days

I'm better at that than others. You'd think that, since sometimes it's more natural to lean on the Lord during a trial, I'd be a pro at that right now. But, you would be wrong.

This process of cancer is not fun nor on the list of things I'd ever like to do again. Though the hardship should make me trust Him each day, that, lamentably, is not the case. Fortunately, I'm brought to my knees in humility when I realize I've been trying to do things on my own once again. When faced with my own need and inability to actually *do* things on my own, I'm back to trusting in Him. Praise the Lord that He loves us in spite of our vacillating all the time between trusting ourselves and trusting Him.

Once again, thank you, thank you, thank you for your love, prayers, and support. God bless, may you stay warm, and may you *know* that His love never ends, His faithfulness is vast, His justice is ever present and deep, and His righteousness is strong and great.

On Christ the solid Rock I stand,

Hannah
Posted at 11:27 p.m.

BACK TO THE START

As I mentioned in the first chapter, Wheaton was not my plan. In fact, I told my parents in high school that I specifically didn't want to go to Wheaton because the only Wheaton grads I knew were teachers, and I did not want to teach. My parents rolled their eyes and chuckled because I knew a grand total of three Wheaton grads, and I knew them because they taught at my small high school. "Just because you go to Wheaton doesn't mean you have to teach, Hannah," my parents laughed. I have an excellent memory, but I cannot, for the life of me, remember why I even applied to Wheaton in the first place since I so adamantly refused to go there. God clearly knew what He was doing. I visited Wheaton in

November of my senior year of high school, but I went solely to appease my parents and get them off my case.

Recently, I hung out with my teammate Stef in her hometown. Stef pointed out a house as we drove around the city. "I was helping my dad paint that house for some cash when I got my acceptance letter to Wheaton," she explained. "I cried when I got in." I laughed because when I received my acceptance letter to Wheaton the day after Christmas of my senior year, I think I said, "Hey guys, I got in to Wheaton," stuffing the letter back into its envelope. My parents were thrilled but I was nonplussed. They kept telling me it was a great school and how it was amazing I'd been accepted, but I just smiled through my teeth, rolled my eyes, and nodded, unconvinced.

When I found out I didn't get in to my dream university one month later, I was crushed. I'd visited multiple times and hung with the volleyball players at camp for two summers, and I genuinely felt like I was supposed to attend the school (and that was the last time I relied on feelings for interpreting God's will) When the shock of my rejection passed and I realized I had to go *somewhere* for college, I chose the best school I got into, Wheaton. I realized then that I needed to visit again because I hadn't taken the first trip in November seriously. My dad and I flew back up to Chicago the last weekend of April before I had to give Wheaton my answer. I was still secretly hoping some school would realize they desperately needed me on their volleyball team, snatching me up at the last minute. I waited until my last possible weekend to visit, and I accepted Wheaton's offer two days before the deadline. I felt resigned to the school because it was second best in my mind.

Wheaton was everything I didn't want. I went to the same private, Christian school from kindergarten through high school graduation, so I wanted to attend a public university with a tangible mission field. Additionally, I wanted to go to a big school with a Division I volleyball program. I hated the cold, so I vowed to avoid it at all costs, and I was ready for an academic program that I could just coast through after enduring a college preparatory curriculum for thirteen years. Wheaton is a small, private, Christian school with rigorous academics. It has a Division III athletic program, and it lies smack in the middle of the frozen tundra of the Midwest. You can see why I dragged my feet heading off to college.

However, Wheaton completely surprised me my freshman year. I had a blast and realized God knew what He was doing. When things became difficult my sophomore year, I tried to convince myself that sometimes God leads us somewhere for a season and then wants us elsewhere (i.e. I was tired of struggling through my challenging year at Wheaton and wanted to be closer to home where it was warm and I wouldn't have to work hard). When transferring fell through and I realized I was stuck at Wheaton, I made my peace with God at the start of my junior year. That year still had its difficulties, but I understood that I needed to fully buy in to God's plan for my life, and for whatever reason, He chose Wheaton. With one semester left and having finally submitted to God's plan for Wheaton, I was way too stubborn to take time off because of cancer. If God had me there and I'd finally gotten on board with His plan, there was no way I was quitting so close to the finish line.

THE WAY PREPARED

In November of my senior year, amidst of all of my medical tests, I had to register for my final semester of college. I thought I only had to take eight hours to graduate, but my dad pointedly told me not to take the path of least resistance, so I planned on a full twelve hour course load for the spring. When the cancer diagnosis arrived, I decided to cut out unnecessary electives, and as I went back to tally up all of my hours, I realized I only had to take five more hours: a four-hour Christian Thought class and a one-hour P.E. credit.

As a freshman, I'd declared psychology as my major. During my sophomore year, in an ironic twist of fate, I had an epiphany during chapel that I was supposed to teach (yep, my biggest fear about Wheaton). I switched to the necessary double major of secondary education and my content area of English. After a year with the double major, I realized it would be impossible for me to graduate on time. Education classes usually included a practicum, and though I spent three hours a week in those practicums, I only received one hour of credit, limiting the number of courses I could take but not compensating me with credit hours. When education professors repeatedly told students the only real way we'd be prepared to teach was by doing it—by experience—I thought, *So I'll graduate late and spend many hours doing work unaccounted for to major in something that won't even help me as much as hands-on experience? Real cool, guys.*

Much to the department's chagrin, I dropped the education major and kept only my English major for my junior and senior years. I didn't want to be lazy, but I had experience managing, mentoring, and teaching kids, having already completed a few practicums, counseling campers during the summers, coaching volleyball teams, and leading high school small groups. The education program was excellent, but I wanted to teach in a private school anyway, so there was little point in going through all the hoops for teacher certification in Illinois public schools when I planned on teaching in Texas private schools (or, ultimately, a Hawaii private school). I could still be a teacher, but I could drop the education major and take more English courses to better know my content area. My peers discouraged the move, but I felt strongly about just keeping the English major. They said things like, "Oh yeah, you're not an education major... what is it you're doing?" or, "Hmm...interesting. Well, good luck!" I really appreciated those votes of confidence.

I entered Wheaton with fifteen hours of credit from deciding on a whim to take three AP courses my senior year of high school. I probably shouldn't have even had that many hours of credit, but when I sat down for the AP Literature in English exam as a high school senior, the main essay prompt centered around *the* quotation from Kate Chopin's book, *The Awakening,* that I wrote my entire fifteen page senior research paper on. Even when I chose *The Awakening* for my research subject as a junior in high school, God was ordering my steps. He knew I'd need credit hours under my belt, and I can only attribute the maximum score of a five I received on the exam to spending my entire senior year writing on the very quotation that formed the AP essay question.

The fact that I had a full semester under my belt entering college, that I had taken sixteen hours almost every semester—including each fall during volleyball season, which is not recommended for an in-season athlete—and that I had dropped the secondary education double major meant I was down to five hours. By my senior year of college, I had seventeen years of private, Christian school under my belt, so I figured if I couldn't pass a Christian Thought class, even during chemo, I didn't deserve to graduate anyway. I was, however, concerned about the P.E. credit because I'd signed up for tennis, and tennis outdoors in the Chicago suburbs from January to March while undergoing chemo seemed physically impossible. I decided I would try to switch to indoor table tennis for my one hour credit, but I had one last hope of getting the credit waived.

As an NCAA athlete and starter on the volleyball team, I thought having to take a one hour P.E. credit seemed illogical. I mean, *really?* Practicing three hours a day, competing in weekly games, and spending every weekend for three months at tournaments didn't exempt me from having to play table tennis or badminton? In the Olympics, those are awesome and highly intense, but at Wheaton, not so much. When I brought that absurdity up to my coach and older teammates, they agreed it was ridiculous but, "That's just how it goes," they told me. Upon being diagnosed with Hodgkin's, I decided I might as well try to pull the cancer card and get out of the credit. I had to meet with the Applied Health Science department chair, and I was nervous because I was going up against a long-established status quo.

However, the professor was in his first year overseeing the department, so he wasn't necessarily set on long-established traditions. When I told him my dilemma and explained that I'd legitimately had my share of physical education over the past four years, the professor told me, "When I was an NCAA swimmer at Syracuse University back in the day, the school waived my credit. I can't believe Wheaton still makes athletes take a one hour P.E. class. I'll sign off on this. Let's call it 'Independent Study Volleyball.'" We negotiated the terms of my release: I had to write a two page paper on how playing volleyball taught me about the relationship between sport and society.

With that, I was down to a four-hour Christian Thought class twice a week and writing a two page paper on volleyball to graduate. That seemed pretty manageable. Despite multiple major changes, worrying at points that I wouldn't graduate on time, and my random scheduling of courses over three and a half years, God had paved the way for my final tumultuous semester. Even more, He had paved the way through my equally whimsical high school choices, unintentionally loading my college schedule for seven semesters, a professor who bunked tradition, and a history of Christian education so I could finish college without missing a beat when my unexpected diagnosis came.

ORDERED STEPS

Beyond academia, I saw even more clearly God knew what He was doing when He dragged me to Wheaton. The chaplain's office prayed for me daily and the student chaplains prayed for me weekly in chapel. My professors read my blog, let me take exams from home, gave me an entire semester extension on my senior English portfolio, and prayed for me faithfully with their families.

One day, I received a letter in my campus mailbox from the president's office. Momentary panic set in because I have a deep-seated fear of getting in trouble. When I opened the letter, I was pleasantly surprised. Wheaton's president simply sent a handwritten letter to tell me he'd heard about my situation and prayer request. Dr. Litfin assured me he was praying for me, reminding me to lean hard on the Lord. In addition, the interim dean of students emailed me, and her message's subject line read, "What can we do for you?" She called me into her office and told me she would talk to my professors, waive my spring semester chapel attendance, and do anything else she could to help me out.

I was floored. I'd done decently well in volleyball, but mostly I stayed below the radar at Wheaton. I like anonymity (surprising given the fact that I'm narrating my life here, but true). I never got to know Wheaton's higher-ups because they intimidated me, but my first interactions with the president, dean of students, and chaplain were incredible, and I was stunned again that God had me in the perfect place. Now, I'm sure my dream school that rejected me is a great university, but had I been there—a big, public, secular institution—I would have had a minimal Christian community; I highly doubt the president would have written me a letter; I'm positive the chaplain's office—much less the entire college—wouldn't be praying for me (since the school didn't have a chaplain); and I doubt I would have been able to graduate from college while fighting cancer.

I'm still amazed when I think about how God had been ordering my steps, bearing with my stubbornness and pride, and leading me unwillingly to the perfect place to face cancer. I'm so thankful He didn't give me my shortsighted high school plans but instead led me exactly where I needed to be. Hindsight's 20/20, and I know without a single doubt I was supposed to attend Wheaton (how sad that it took me until my last semester of college to see what God had been doing all along).

The movie *Signs* has a scene paralleling how I felt (cue spoiler alert). Mel Gibson's character Graham is a bitter single dad raising his two children with the help of his brother Merrill, a former minor-league baseball player with a record for the most strikes because he always wanted to swing at the ball. Graham is mourning his wife's death, which was caused by a driver who fell asleep at the wheel, and the incident has caused him to walk away from his faith. His young daughter Bo is quirky and has an irritating habit of leaving half-filled water glasses all over the house because she fears the water becomes contaminated. His son Morgan has fairly severe asthma, so Graham has a lot on his hands. Some aliens threaten to invade earth, only adding to his angst in life, as you can imagine.

In the climactic scene of the movie, an alien holds his son (who's suffered an asthma attack), and threatens to inject him with poison as Graham, Merrill, and Bo stand by, frozen. Graham flashes back to the scene of the car crash that pinned his wife to a tree, leaving her mortally wounded but conscious just long enough to say goodbye to her husband. She says, "Tell him to see, and tell Merrill to swing away." At the time, Graham assumed the strange advice was due to her neurons firing randomly because of the trauma she sustained, thus the third person reference to her husband to whom she's speaking. But as Graham returns to the present, squared off against the threatening alien, he realizes she was prescient, leaving him words for the future.

Graham "sees" Merrill's record breaking baseball bat mounted on the wall, and tells him, "Swing away," and Merrill catches his drift, remembering those last words. The alien sprays his poison into Morgan's nostrils as Merrill grabs the bat and attacks the alien. Merrill gains the advantage when one of Bo's water glasses spills on the alien, acting like acid on its skin. Just then, dad and daughter exchange a knowing look, as if this—*this*—is the reason for her irrational fear of contaminated water. Graham leaves Merrill to finish off the alien by swinging away at all of those water glasses, and he grabs Morgan's limp body, taking his son and Bo outside to the front lawn.

Graham realizes that, although Morgan's asthma attack was hazardous because it constricted his airways, it prevented the alien's poison from entering his lungs. Graham mutters aloud in disbelief, "That's why he had asthma—it can't be luck. His lungs were closed; no poison got in." Merrill joins the trio outside after defeating the alien while Graham is overcome by emotion from the situation. An earlier conversation with

Merrill replays in his mind in which Graham said, "...what you have to ask yourself is what kind of person are you? Are you the kind who sees signs—sees miracles—or do you believe that people just get lucky? Is it possible there are no coincidences?" Though earlier Graham in bitterness had chalked it all up to randomness, now he sits on the ground outside of his home, completely dumbfounded and restored to his faith because everything cosmically aligns and finally makes sense in this moment.

Writer Henry James calls these moments of understanding "backward clearness...when [we] read the past in the light of the present...."[11] Much like Graham from *Signs*, I experienced backward clearness during my final semester of college. *Oh, that's what God was doing!* All of these elements—the full semester of credit from my high school AP exams, the solo English major, the adjusted P.E. credit, the waived chapel attendance, my one Christian Thought course, being at Wheaton—came together at the perfect moment to show me that God had prepared my path all along. He hadn't been punishing me or carelessly disregarding my desires. He had a greater plan, and though I fought it at just about every stage, He patiently loved me through it, showing how utterly faithful and sovereign He is. Everything made sense all at once.

I realize that might sound melodramatic. Compared to a family cosmically protected from attacking aliens, Hollywood-style, my story seems lame, but I felt as if a light had broken through, giving me an "aha" moment and revealing God at work. I don't believe people just get lucky, and my experience with cancer reinforced my belief that there are no coincidences, only steps ordered by a faithful and sovereign God.

God promises all throughout His Word that He is faithful and has perfect plans for our lives, but though I always read those words and agree, I take a while to believe them wholeheartedly. I'm guessing I'm not the only one, either. We may not always see what He's doing as it happens, and we may never get to see on this side of Heaven. But, when God has shown me glimpses of His plan, all I can do is thank Him and stand amazed at His sovereignty. God's plan greatly surpasses anything I could ever concoct. Seeing how He had provided for me to complete chemo while finishing college at Wheaton helped me remember daily that if God had so proven His faithfulness by preparing the way thus far, He would carry me through cancer, which somehow also fit into His perfect plan.

You might read this and think, *Oh, isn't that just precious and nice that everything worked out so perfectly for Hannah. Meanwhile, my life kinda sucks right now.* I don't share this to say my life is picture perfect; in fact, most of the time, I'm the one looking around wondering how things seem to work out so nicely for others while I feel like I can't get a break. I share this to encourage you that, even if we can't possibly see the bigger picture, even if we stubbornly resist where He's leading us every step of the way, and even if we bitterly resent where He has us now, God is still sovereign. He knows what He's doing, and He is way bigger than our pride, our foolishness, our terrible discernment, our fears, our cancer, and our trials.

GOD'S IMPECCABLE TIMING

God also showed He had faithfully prepared my way through cancer medically. In her child life specialist internship, my sister Katie had wrapped up an oncology unit just weeks before my Christmas shopping was so rudely interrupted with that call. She knew about all different types of cancer and chemotherapy regimens; she actually had a binder full of information on cancer. After discussing my symptoms with her supervising doctors, she called my dad and told him she thought I had stage II Hodkgin's lymphoma (though my attorney dad had already come to the same conclusion based on his highly scientific research on WebMD). We joke about how Katie—and, of course, my dad— diagnosed me correctly, but really by the time Dr. Santi called to confirm I had cancer, Katie's preeminent briefing had somewhat prepared me to accept the worst.

As part of her job in bridging the gaps between doctors and patients, Katie sits down with sick children's parents to explain the ins and outs of diagnoses and answer questions. Since she'd just learned how to confront parents with the news of cancer, Katie sat my parents down at our kitchen table and gave them her child life specialist talk, briefing them on what I faced, how I'd need help, and what they could do for me. Additionally, Katie has to know about all kinds of medications and drug interactions for her job, so when I had questions about whether I could take certain medications but didn't want to bother my doctors late at night, I called my sister. If she didn't know, she'd ask her doctor friends and get back to me. Katie's internship couldn't have come at a better time, and we're certain it wasn't a coincidence.

Our health insurance is another clue that something more than chance was at work. My dad and his law partner have owned their firm for over twenty years, and those guys are creatures of habit, so if something isn't broken, they sure as heck aren't fixing it. Their law firm had subscribed to the same health insurer since the firm's origins. However, nine months before my cancer diagnosis, one day in March my dad's office manager stopped by to tell him they received an offer from a new insurer, Blue Cross Blue Shield. They received offers like that from time to time, but no one ever paid them any heed. Thus, my dad cannot, for the life of him, tell you why he so uncharacteristically told Pam, "Sure, let's do it! Let's switch."

Being typically methodical and Type A, he looks back and can't think of one logical reason he agreed to up and switch the whole firm and their family members' health insurance. In fact, switching was a major pain because they'd had the same insurer for so long. After that decision, anytime employees or family members went to the doctor, they had to fill out those annoying change of insurance forms. On top of that, my dad can't explain his reasoning for the change because with Blue Cross, they now pay a higher premium than with their previous insurer.

In the chaos of trying to find an oncologist in November and then learning from the Friedls that Dr. Gordon would meet with me, my parents and I overlooked one important detail: insurance. We focused so much on finding a doctor that we never checked to see whether Northwestern even accepted our insurance. When we hung up with the Friedls and went upstairs to learn more about the hospital and Dr. Gordon, we realized we'd been too hasty. My parents and I timidly got on the computer and went to the hospital's website, crossing our fingers that they took our insurance. A minute later, the information page loaded. They accepted Blue Cross but not our previous insurer. My dad proceeded to explain the back story for his seemingly illogical decision in March. He added that, despite the higher premium, Blue Cross would cover 100% beyond the deductible whereas the previous company only covered 80%. When paying for expensive bills like cancer treatment, that 20% quickly adds up and can cost more than a cheaper premium.

We were floored. God in His faithfulness used a passing moment in my dad's office when he uncharacteristically made an impulsive decision to provide for us nine months later when, out of the blue, I was diagnosed with cancer. Insurance might seem like a minor detail, but to me, it's one more reminder that God is never surprised though things sneak up on us in life. Though nine months earlier—even one month earlier—we couldn't have fathomed someone in the family being diagnosed with cancer, God knew and was preparing the way all along.

My greatest comfort in any situation is that, though life may blindside me (I mean, finding out I had cancer in the middle of a mall was pretty bizarre), God is not suddenly scrambling, trying to figure out what to do. He's known all along, and though my world seems unstable, God is still seated on His throne.

We have to trust that God is sovereign and for whatever reason knew our trials would better, rather than worsen, our character. One of my favorite quotes by Wiersbe in his commentary on Psalms says, "When pondering the mysteries of life, hold on to what you know for sure, and never doubt in the darkness what God has taught you in the light."[12] I recently found out that Wheaton College's fourth president, Victor Raymond Edman—for whom Wheaton's chapel is named—is credited with saying that, a poignant fact, given the meaningful time I spent in that chapel. In the light, I know without a doubt God loves me and is sovereign, that He is "close to the brokenhearted" whether I feel it or not (Psalm 34:18). When walking through cancer and other seasons of darkness, I have had to cling to and fall back on that truth. I can't doubt in the rough seasons what I know so plainly to be true in those moments of light. We can't forget those truths when the nights get long and the days turn colder. Instead, we have to remember what we learned in the light: God loves us, He is sovereign, He has plans far greater than our wildest dreams, and He is right beside us whether we feel Him or not.

REST IN HIS SOVEREIGNTY

In late February about halfway through my treatments, one of my aunts sent me the book *Through Gates of Splendor* by Elisabeth Elliot in a chemo care package. I was familiar with the book because Elisabeth and her husband Jim graduated from Wheaton. Jim was one of the five missionaries killed while serving in Ecuador in the 1950s. The movie by the same name came out when I was in college, and though I'd meant to see the film, I never did. So when I opened my care package, I was excited to see the book inside. In periods of sleeplessness, I watched TV or did some pleasure reading, so one night I picked up Elliot's book. Near her conclusion, she reflects on the significance of the deaths of her husband and his four missionary friends. Elliot writes, "God is God. If He is God, He is worthy of my worship and my service. I will find rest nowhere but in His will, and that will is infinitely, immeasurably, unspeakably beyond my largest notions of what He is up to."[13]

Now, my situation didn't even come close to comparing with her story and the tragedy those men and their widows faced. But God promises that, no matter what situation we face, He will provide for us and give each of us exactly what we need to draw near to Him and bring Him glory. Ultimately, I needed to surrender to the fact that God is God, and I am quite simply not. Singer Steven Curtis Chapman echoes Elliot's sentiment in a song aptly titled "God is God." He sings, "God is God and I am not. I can only see a part of the picture He's painting. God is God and I am man. So I'll never understand it all, for only God is God."[14] Both of them speak to what Job finally understood and what we have to come to terms with: God is sovereign, and we are not. And since He is sovereign, He is worthy of our worship, our service, and our lives. We can only see a small part of what He's doing in and through our lives, but His will is "infinitely, immeasurably, unspeakably beyond my largest notions of what He is up to."

Each time I've seen even a fraction of what God's been up to and how everything falls so perfectly into place, I am overwhelmed with His immense sovereignty and perfect plan. My plans rarely turn out how I envision. I legitimately felt like I was supposed to attend my dream college, but I was flat rejected—I wasn't even wait-listed. In high school I dreamed of playing Division I volleyball but got kicked off my club team for standing up for my faith during the most important recruiting season, so I missed my chance. I thought I could finally kick back and relax, coasting through my senior year at Wheaton, but I was diagnosed with cancer. I felt God's prompting to write this book, so I quit my job in Hawaii and moved back home to Texas. I've started to expect the unexpected.

Although my plans rarely come to fruition, God's plans are so much greater than I ever could have imagined. And, as Elliot affirms, the only place to rest is in His will anyway. God works way outside of our limited scope, and during cancer, I realized I'm okay if the Lord leads me down an unexpected path because He knows what He's doing. Do I think getting cancer was fair? Not really. Do I understand it? Not completely. But do I doubt God's faithfulness? No. Absolutely not.

After my final treatment at the end of May, I stopped off for a few days at Kanakuk in Lampe, Missouri to break up my final fifteen hour drive home from college. It was staff training week, and one of the annual highlights was worship night before the kids came the following day. This year was so different for me. Not only was I not on staff this summer, but I was also wearing a wig, I'd just survived my final chemo treatment, and I felt like I'd been hit by a semi truck. However, that year's worship night stands out in my mind as more poignant than the previous three when I was actually on staff. As we sang "Whom Have I But You?" by David Ruis, I started getting choked up as I thought about the words. They're simple but poignant, and I love them: "Whom have I but You? Though the mountains fall, they fall into the sea. Whom have I but You? Whom have I but You? Though my colored dawn may turn to shades of gray. Whom have I but You? Whom have I but You? Though the questions asked may never be resolved. Whom have I but You?"[15]

When we came to the final verse, "though the questions asked may never be resolved," I realized those words summed up my life lately. Though my world started to crumble, though my colored dawn turned darker, and though I may never actually get an answer to why I had cancer—though all of those things hovered in my mind, I could claim so surely then and still today, *Whom have I but Jesus Christ?*

THE RED SEA RULES

One day midway through treatment, I came home from class and found a small package on my front porch. I thought my aunts had missed the memo because I was between chemo treatments, but then I saw that the padded envelope was from a woman named Vicki. My dad grew up knowing Vicki, and my mom attended Bible study with her in college, but my parents didn't connect that they both knew her until they had dated for a while. I've heard about her all of my life but only met her recently. Inside the package was a brief note and a small hardback book titled *The Red Sea Rules* by Robert J. Morgan. In her note, Vicki explained she'd received the book when her mom was diagnosed with breast cancer, and it helped her immensely when she passed away.

Curious to find out more, I began reading. In the book, Morgan outlines ten different rules he's found to be true, both in Israel's history and in his own experiences with difficult times. The first rule is, "Realize that God means for you to be where you are." Morgan explains, "When you are in a difficult place, realize that the Lord either placed you there or allowed you to be there, for reasons perhaps known for now only to Himself. The same God who led you *in* will lead you *out*."[16] Nothing we go through is outside of God's vision, so we have to accept the fact—hard as it may be—that God has a reason for either placing us here or allowing us to be placed here. But, the enduring comfort is the same God who led us into this trial will also lead us out.

Think about the Israelites. They were perennial complainers. If you haven't caught that by now, it's time to brush up on your Old Testament reading. What amazes me most about their doubt God would save them is that they *walked through the Red Sea on dry ground*. Furthermore, once they were safely to the other side, they watched the water crash back down, drowning their Egyptian enemies. How do people see God physically part the ocean for them, walk through said ocean without getting wet, and then question whether God will let them die in the wilderness or not? Every time I read their complaints, "Did God save us just to let us die in the desert?" I want to smack them back to reality (Exodus 16:3, 17:3). *Seriously? If He cares enough about you to split an ocean, I'm pretty sure He's going to get you out of the desert as He promised,* I want to tell them.

I say that, and yet, I am no different from the Israelites. How many times have I seen God's amazing faithfulness only to doubt it when I hit a new trial? If God had so clearly prepared the way for me and my family through cancer by lining up our insurance, doctors, a treatment plan enabling me to graduate from college and finish chemo four days later, and so many more details, how on earth could I doubt He would be sovereign in the future? Yet, I *have* doubted Him and whether He'll take care of the details since then.

We have to remember when walking through trials that the same God who brought us in will bring us out. How He brings us out won't look identical in every case. Some may have to take a semester off of school, go on disability at work, or find that treatment isn't working. But God is faithful, and if He pays such close attention to us that He knows the number of hairs on our heads, there's no chance God will somehow forget He led us into a trial (Matthew 10:30). He will bring us out, turning our "darkness into light" (Psalm 18:28). God has always rescued His people, and He will always rescue them and turn darkness into light. It might not look how we envision a rescue to play out—all warm, comfy, and happily ever after with a new castle to go home to—but God is still sovereign.

THROUGH THE FIRE

I grew up knowing the story of Shadrach, Meshach, and Abednego in the book of Daniel, but somehow, the story became commonplace to me over the years. Only as I've gotten older have I truly seen what an amazing story it is. I love the trio's unwavering trust in God. In Daniel 3:16-18, Shadrach, Meshach, and Abednego reply to the king's threat that he will throw them into a furnace if they don't bow down and worship him. They say, "O Nebuchadnezzar, we do not need to defend ourselves before you in this matter. If we are thrown into the blazing furnace, the God we serve is able to save us from it, and He will rescue us from your hand, O king. *But even if He does not*, we want you to know, O king, that we will not serve your gods or worship the image of gold you have set up" (emphasis mine).

What faith they had: faith that God could and would rescue them from the furnace, but more strikingly, faith that even if He didn't save them, God was still sovereign and they would not bow down. They probably sounded crazy. Who literally heads into a furnace of fire and walks out unscathed? But they knew God could do such a miracle. They understood God would rescue them either way: physically from the furnace, or, if they perished within, He would rescue them eternally and bring them to Himself.

No matter what stage of cancer or situation in life we face, I think we have to say: *God, I know You have all power to save me from this. But even if You don't, I will not swerve to the right or left; I will continue to love, serve, and trust You.*

We don't have to like our circumstances. I'm pretty sure Shadrach, Meshach, and Abednego weren't clapping their hands and cheering, thrilled to be walking into a fiery oven. I highly doubt when the apostle Paul wrote to the Philippians, he was living it up, enjoying prison. But, here's what he realized: "Now I want you to know, brothers, that what has happened to me has really served to advance the gospel. As a result, it has become clear throughout the whole palace guard and to everyone else that I am in chains for Christ. Because of my chains, most of the brothers in the Lord have been encouraged to speak the word of God more courageously and fearlessly" (Philippians 1:12-14).

Though his situation wasn't ideal, Paul realized God was at work, and he praised Him. We need to see God through the fire, praying and believing He will use our circumstances for His glory. Even though we may not feel equipped to walk through life's trials, we have to trust that God has been preparing us for them since long before we heard the bad news. No matter the situation, God is God, and we are not. He is sovereign. If we can accept that, His peace will dwell in our hearts.

In the Word:

- **1 Chronicles 29:11-12** "Everything in the heavens and earth is Yours oh Lord, and this is Your kingdom. We adore You as being in control of everything. Riches and honor come from You alone and You are the ruler of all mankind. Your hand controls power and might and it is at Your discretion that men are made great and given strength!"
- **Psalm 34:17-20** "The righteous cry out, and the Lord hears them; He delivers them from all their troubles. The Lord is close to the brokenhearted and saves those who are crushed in spirit. A righteous man may have many troubles, but the Lord delivers him from them all; He protects all his bones, not one of them will be broken."
- **Psalm 62:1-2** "My soul finds rest in God alone; my salvation comes from Him. He alone is my rock and my salvation; He is my fortress, I will never be shaken."
- **Psalm 89:8-9** "O Lord God Almighty, who is like You? You are mighty, O Lord, and Your faithfulness surrounds You. You rule over the surging sea; when its waves mount up, You still them."
- **Isaiah 26:3-4** "You will keep in perfect peace him whose mind is steadfast because he trusts in You. Trust in the Lord forever, for the Lord, the Lord, is the Rock eternal."
- **1 John 4:4** "You, dear children, are from God and have overcome them, because the One who is in you is greater than the one who is in the world."

Recommended Reading:

- *The Red Sea Rules* by Robert J. Morgan can be found online at Barnes and Noble and Amazon. It's a brief book, an easy read, and one of the most encouraging and helpful truths I've ever read.
- *Through Gates of Splendor* by Elisabeth Elliot is a great read about the five missionaries who were killed in Ecuador in the 1950s and Elliot's ruminations on God's faithfulness and sovereignty through life's trials.

CHAPTER 8

Finding the Victories

Tuesday, March 17, 2009

"We went through fire and water, but You brought us to a place of abundance" (Psalm 66:12b).

Happy St. Patrick's Day! Today is officially an amazing day because it is 75 degrees outside and sunny, too (yes, in Wheaton, IL in *March*)! Plus, I am still energized from having an amazing spring break in NYC with my Kanakuk co-counselor Melissa last week.

However, I'll be really honest with you: I'm tired of this whole chemo thing. It's pretty lame, in my opinion. Currently, I can't straighten my left arm due to the effects of the drugs on my veins which make my arm really painful and my veins ropey (if that's actually a word). Also, I have one vein so tight I'm convinced if I do straighten my left arm, the vein might actually snap in half.

My perseverance is being tested, so for those of you who are praying for resolve, thank you! That said, I have seen lately— through encouragement, reminders of God's faithfulness, and hearing about other people battling intense cancers and other hardships—that I am so blessed in this journey, no matter how my sarcastic and slightly pessimistic self might otherwise tend to believe.

That's the report from me now. I'd like to close with an excerpt from a book my mom's sisters gave her in one of the chemo day care packages they so faithfully send for each treatment. My mom passed on the book *Same Kind of Different as Me* by Ron Hall and Denver Moore, and while I'm usually slow to read trendy Christian books (call me a literature snob or simply stubborn), I'm putting my literary stamp of endorsement on this one. Keep some tissues with you, though. I had to stop reading it on the airplane to New York because I think the man next to me was getting concerned about me. It's a great story of two men from completely different worlds, how they end up forming a relationship, and what happens along the way. Read it.

Here's something Ron Hall writes at the end of the book as he's reflecting upon this unexpected journey he's been on, talking about the pain and tears he still has (I'll try not to give too much away):

And I cannot mask my disappointment that God did not answer yes to our prayers.,, I think He's okay with that. One of the phrases we evangelicals like to throw around is that Christianity is "not just a religion; it's a relationship." I believe that, which is why I know that when my faith was shattered and I raged against Him, He still accepted me. And even though I have penciled a black mark in His column, I can be honest about it. That's what a relationship is all about.[17]

You may or may not agree with his words, but when I read that statement at the end of the book, it resonated so greatly with me. My situation is nowhere near as hard to handle as Ron's and so many others'. Nevertheless, I understand feeling disappointed that God has not answered "Yes" to many prayers over the past six months. What's more, I have definitely been learning what Ron says next. He thinks God's okay with us being disappointed that He hasn't answered certain prayers in ways we'd like.

As bad as that may initially sound, my faith *is*, in fact, about a relationship, and since God knows how I'm actually feeling deep down inside, there's no point acting like I'm happy with dumb cancer or like I'm excited He said "No" to a prayer. That's not real, and from my experience, that's groundwork for a pretty lame relationship.

Furthermore, I like that Ron talked about "penciling a black mark in that column," because I feel like doing that at times, and I'm glad I'm not the only one! I know through and through that God is faithful, and I am absolutely sure His plans for me are so much better than I could imagine, but that doesn't mean I'm always happy about them or I forget my disappointment. I wish I could forget the stinging disappointment I felt in high school when my dream college rejected me, but, even in that now-insignificant time, I think I probably penciled a black mark in the column of prayers answered other than how I wanted. What's most important about all of my rambling is that, since my walk *is* a relationship with God, as Ron says, I can be honest about my disappointment, and God won't suddenly un-accept me when I'm honest.

Two things: (1) I am so thankful we have a dynamic relationship with God and that He's okay with me being me: cynical at times, sarcastic most of the time, and a glorious mess all the time, and (2) you really should read *Same Kind of Different as Me*.

On Christ the solid Rock I stand,

Hannah
Posted at 3:18 p.m.

I got used to my wigs and the routine of chemo, and before I knew it, January rolled into February. I returned to the hospital after my fourth treatment to redo all of my staging tests and scans to see whether the chemo was working or not. Five days later, I was home for a long weekend driving around Texas when my phone lit up. My nurse practitioner Sarah Miyata was calling, so I answered the phone and held my breath. Sarah said she was calling to tell me the tests came back negative and I was in remission. She sounded upbeat, and I was pretty sure remission was a good thing, but I'd heard way too many cancer terms thrown around to make assumptions (e.g. malignant, benign, remission, etc.). Plus, "Your scans came back negative" is pretty poor wording to mean everything's fine, so I made sure to verify what I thought. I asked, "So....that means there's no cancer, right?" Sarah confirmed that remission means free from cancer and negative scans mean "negative for" or clear of cancer.

When I passed the good news on to my friends and family members, many said, "Wow, you're done after only four treatments!" Unfortunately, I had to explain, that was not the case. My first four chemo treatments had poisoned off the cancer cells, but I still had to go through eight more to completely destroy any potential cancer cells, clearing me for the future. I wasn't off the hook, but since I'd first heard the word "biopsy" back in November, Sarah's call that sunny February day was the first victory I'd had in a long time. *About time!* I thought. That remission call also marked the first time anyone knew whether treatment was even working or not. Thankfully, it was. After four treatments, I realized I still had a long way to go, but I found that right when I started to feel daunted, God provided. With the victory of remission, I found renewed energy for the next few treatments. But, like the Israelites who seem to always get stuck in bad cycles, my enthusiasm started to wane again as February turned to March, so I had to remind myself God had given me that victory and many others along the way, even though "cancer" and "victory" seem mutually exclusive.

IN NEED OF A VICTORY

I've alluded to the fact that the months leading up to my diagnosis were challenging, so let me explain. It all started in the spring when I acquired stitches from the malfunctioning volleyball pole that caused me to, once again, sit out of practice. Then I had an awkward relationship talk with one of my closest guy friends and we hadn't talked since, plus a new friend had a meltdown on me, and drama isn't my thing, so I didn't know what to do about her. Though my junior year had been great, I was ready for summer and excited about the next thing, working at Kanakuk Kamps. The previous two summers had been some of the best times of my life as I was surrounded by friends, pouring into middle school girls, and encouraged by godly men and women. I attended Kanakuk for twelve summers growing up, and then in college, I was a counselor there for three more. For fifteen of my twenty-one years, Kanakuk had been a regular part of life.

But soon after arriving for staff training, I realized this summer would be different. Most of my friends from the previous two summers had moved on, and I missed them. Many other counselors were coming off of their freshman year of college full of life and fairly clueless, while I was heading into my senior year, coming to terms with the daunting prospect of graduating and growing up, so I felt old and out of place. While most cabins had two counselors, one of the staff members asked me to lead and help train some counselors, so I was paired with two co-counselors. We all know two's company and three's a crowd...especially when you're in charge of twelve exhausting middle school girls with emotions running high. I tried to lead my co-counselors and all of our campers, but I didn't feel successful in that endeavor.

A few other factors combined to taint the experience, and suddenly I found myself confronted with the reality that my time at Kanakuk was probably coming to an end. I absolutely loved all the summers I spent there, and the camp has shaped who I am possibly more than any other influence, so I'm thankful for it. I'm nostalgic and sentimental, so I hate saying goodbye, and facing the truth that this was my final summer at camp was hard, especially for it to end on such a bittersweet note.

The whole experience bummed me out, but I pressed on, focusing on the next goal: my upcoming senior season of Wheaton volleyball. I would be a captain, and it was a rebuilding year, so I eagerly anticipated the opportunity to lead the girls to success and help shape the program. But because of multiple injuries, some conflict between other players, and situations out of my control, the season didn't turn out like that. Then when volleyball ended, I started seeing doctors about my lymph nodes.

Life seemed to be rocking along smoothly for everyone else, but I felt like I was sustaining hit after hit, wondering, *Can't I just get a break?*

In November right after my team failed to make it to the conference tournament for the first time in my college career, I called my best friend and Kanakuk co-counselor Melissa. At the time, she was in graduate school for counseling, living with my sister Katie in Atlanta. Melissa has always had great insight, and she is a kindred spirit with whom I can share everything. I tried to hold all of my emotions together after such a disappointing few months, but as I told her in exasperation, "I just need a *victory* right now!" I burst into tears. Our conversation is so vivid to me, and I remember feeling so frustrated with my circumstances and seeming disappointment after disappointment. She remembers that call, too, and she was encouraging as always as we talked.

Two weeks later, I was diagnosed with cancer.

Two nights before Melissa got married, we stayed up and had one last pillow talk as single girls. Our conversation returned to that phone call. I told her how distinct it was in my memory and how crazy it was that two weeks later I was diagnosed with cancer. The only reason I didn't fall apart in disappointment was because God carried me. That was definitely not the victory I wanted; on the contrary, cancer seemed more like another failure than success. However, Melissa and I reflected that my cancer actually *was* a victory—a different one than I'd been wanting, but better than I could have imagined.

In *The Princess Diaries*, there's a scene in which the main character Mia Thermopolis and her best friend Lilly Moscovitz talk about needing a miracle. In light of Mia's dissatisfaction with the recent revelation that she's a princess, her best friend Lilly calls her out saying, "You being a princess is kind of a miracle...What *more* of a miracle could you want?" Mia replies, "We'll have to find a different miracle. Not *more*, just *different*," trying to avoid her royal destiny and all. I felt like Mia, but instead of a miracle, I needed a victory. I appreciated each time someone told me how I was changing his or her life, but that wasn't exactly my idea of success. I didn't want *more* of a victory; I wanted a *different* one, one that didn't involve cancer.

Underlying my frustration with the string of disappointments was the more acute frustration that everything I poured myself into seemed to come up empty, leaving me nothing to show for it. I felt like I really hadn't made an impact, like Wheaton College, Thunder Volleyball, Kanakuk, K-Life, and anything else I had a hand in would be no different without me. That was a disheartening prospect when I'd poured myself into my endeavors. Bummer. So, I called Melissa, sobbed to her, and in frustration whined about just needing a victory. By "needing a victory," I meant that I wanted to get recognition in volleyball or have some great job fall into my lap—something shortsighted, something that made me feel affirmed, and ultimately something much smaller than the victory God would provide through cancer.

But isn't that usually how it is? Doesn't God usually have amazing plans for us? While we're plotting and planning down here on earth in very shortsighted and small ways, He's telling us to simply trust Him and let Him do something so much greater than we could ever imagine. God knew the better victory I needed wasn't to leave a mark in the volleyball record book; He knew that I needed to know I'd made a mark in people's lives and that He was using me for His kingdom.

When I was diagnosed with cancer, I was overwhelmed by the tears people cried for me. Obviously God knew I needed encouragement and to see that I was, in fact, impacting people despite my volleyball win/loss record, despite whether I was the perfect Kanakuk counselor or not, and despite those relationships that didn't turn out so well. It was a different victory than I ever pictured. I was daily reminded how many people loved, cared for, and supported me, and for that, I am eternally grateful. It began to dawn on me that I had a big impact on people that I never anticipated. I think a lot of people probably don't get to witness that—I certainly hadn't before. At funerals people share how much the deceased has meant to them, but rarely in life do people tell others how impactful they've been. I was floored, and I still am as I see that while I complained about not making an impact and just wanted to give up, God had to be shaking His head, whispering, "If you'll just wait, Hannah, you'll see."

CANCER: A BLESSING?

On one of my better days toward the end of treatment, I felt well enough to be out, about, and running errands, so I stopped by a few different stores, ending my day's excursions at a Christian bookstore. I perused the shelves trying to find something to read in all of my down time, and I saw a table featuring recent releases. One was titled *The Great Eight*,[18] and the author's name caught my eye: Scott Hamilton. I started figure skating when I was three years old and competed until I was thirteen. I'm not sure who thought that was a good idea since all throughout my childhood I was off the charts in height and not stick-skinny, but I'm sure I learned something from those ten years...at least I hope so. I grew up watching Scott perform his signature back flips on the ice, but I hadn't known he was a believer. I did know he'd battled a brain tumor, so I was intrigued and bought his autobiography.

Once the cynic in me got over his figure skating analogies for life, I found he had some really good thoughts. Since the guy went through cancer and then years later a totally unrelated brain tumor, I feel like Scott has the experience from which to speak. He writes that so many different times, he probably should have been miserable by the world's standards. If he had stepped back to assess the situation, he's sure he would have been bitter and frustrated. But ironically, he talked about how, while cancer was the worst thing that had ever happened to him, it was also the best thing that had ever happened to him.

I read Scott's autobiography around chemo treatments nine and ten, and those were pretty rough times. When Scott first said cancer was the best thing he'd ever been through, I figured his brain tumor must have affected his cognitive reasoning and sanity. *Really? The best thing you've ever gone through? Even though you almost died...twice? Even though you felt terrible for years? Even though cancer took a great emotional and physical toll?* At that point, I was sick of cancer, sick of chemo, and sick of feeling sick. Scott seemed so upbeat about his cancer while I felt like I was fighting just to keep my head above water. *Yep,* I decided, *Scott Hamilton must be crazy.* I put the book down for a few days, but I couldn't shake that idea. Scott had been joyful when he should have been miserable because cancer, while difficult, was the best thing that had ever happened.

After mulling the thought over for a while, I admitted Scott had a point. At the time, I sure as heck didn't think cancer was the best thing that had ever happened to me, but even amidst the most difficult experience of my life and during the treatments when I started to lose my hope and resolve, I recognized that cancer had already shown God's blessings in great ways. The unexpected and overabundant support I received from friends, family members, and even random strangers was enough to make me realize that, despite this challenging time, I was blessed and God was good.

I'm not saying I was ready to claim cancer as the greatest experience of my life quite yet, but even amidst feeling crappy all the time, it was overwhelmingly clear God was at work and showing me victories as I glimpsed His love and His people's love for me. Friends who had let me down in the past were some of the most faithful to check in on me, pray for me, and send me random treats. Campers of mine told me how much I encouraged them, and a couple of people told me I was their hero. Without cancer, I'm not sure any of those things would have happened. Seeing so clearly the goodness of God's people—broken and all—made the challenging experience of cancer a blessing in disguise. Now when I look back, I, too, see cancer as one of the most meaningful and best experiences of my life, exactly as Scott asserted.

Not only did I learn to trust others and ask for help, but I found a huge victory in the depth of my relationships. I lived with two of my best friends and teammates during my dreadful sophomore year, and all three of us would say the living arrangements were...well...challenging, for lack of a better word. We were together at volleyball practice, games, and tournaments, we had the same friends outside of volleyball, and we even had some of the same classes. We all know that familiarity breeds contempt. I'm pretty independent, and while I love the freedom that brings, it also has its drawbacks; namely, I need space and me time. Being together all the time started to drive me crazy, and on top of my shoulder pain and its resulting insomnia, I was not a happy, shiny person to live with. My relationship with Mallory and Annie took a major hit that year, some of it due to unforeseen circumstances, but most of it due to my selfishness. During our junior year, we started to rebuild our relationships, but always present was the bitter memory of how poorly we'd treated each other and how something felt lost.

When I was diagnosed with cancer, our relationships changed again, but for the better. Mallory and I had a great heart to heart about things six months after we graduated from college as we reflected back to the different stages of our relationship. After we both admitted we'd been selfish and immature as roommates, all was forgiven, and we laughed at how it took three years to see with such clarity and own up to our ridiculousness. What was really clear, though, was that all had been forgiven during our senior year. Though we'd still been recovering from a best friend relationship gone wrong, it was as if, in light of cancer, none of that really mattered. Because honestly, it didn't. Cancer helped me put things in perspective. Given that I was going through chemo, had to shave my head, and fought death, my petty roommate squabbles with Mallory and Annie two years earlier were completely irrelevant.

That proved true in most of my other relationships as well. Cancer changed them, and definitely for the better. I didn't have the energy to bicker with my sisters, and in survival mode, no one cared about the dumb issues we'd harped on in earlier days. My relationship with my parents grew much deeper, my teammates became less like colleagues on the court and more like sisters, and the Armstrongs moved from being my friends' parents to my second family. If cancer could do all that, then I definitely call cancer a victory.

PURPOSE IN THE STRUGGLE

I get easily discouraged, not because I need people to tell me that I'm awesome or anything, but because I need to know that what I'm doing is making a difference. It's something I'm working on—staying encouraged and remembering my purpose in what I'm doing. I think that's where I found myself before I heard my diagnosis. I lost sight of my goal, grew disheartened, and needed some encouragement that, even in the face of disappointment, I still had a purpose. Cancer didn't exactly seem to affirm that I was doing a good job with what God had given me.

Commenting on Psalm 6:7-10, Wiersbe writes:

> Sometimes God chastens us to deal with our disobedience, but at other times, He chastens us to prepare us for what lies ahead. It's like the training of an athlete for a race. David thought God was angry with him, but that wasn't necessarily true. However, when you consider that he was surrounded by foes, evildoers, and enemies and that his body was weak and in pain and his soul troubled, you can see why he felt like he had a target on his back.[19]

I resonated with the psalms in which David cries out that he hasn't done wrong and can't see why God has brought certain trials into his life. I mean, I knew I wasn't perfect, and I wasn't claiming to be, but I'd been genuinely seeking the Lord and trying to walk in His way, so I didn't think cancer was some sort of punishment for my sin. However, on the days when I felt terrible, grew disheartened, and lost hope, I started to examine my life, wondering if this was somehow a judgment on my character. I was like Job who maintains his innocence to his wife and friends, but when he starts to examine his life and what God is doing, he questions God's plan and wonders if he's in the wrong.

When those thoughts cross our minds, we have to remember Wiersbe's encouragement. Cancer and other trials aren't necessarily judgments on our lives. God isn't on our case. On the contrary, He is very much on our side. Sometimes we go through the hard periods of life like an athlete preparing for a race. Sometimes we need difficult practices, pain and sore muscles, and times that aren't fluid to be able to do our best come race time. I started running a couple of years ago, and I trained for and ran my first half marathon a little over a year ago. While the training was painful, required me to run outside in winter weather, and at times made me want to give up, when race day rolled around, I was so thankful for the difficult months of training. I had the mental preparation, stamina, and experience needed to run the race under my goal time.

Though many times in the Old and New Testaments, sickness is invariably tied to sin, in John 9:1-3, Jesus counters that link as He discusses the man born blind. "'Neither this man nor his parents sinned,' said Jesus, 'but this happened that the work of God would be displayed in his life.'" Though it may not sound so fun to us, God can use our sicknesses to further His kingdom and display His work in our lives, and that is an eternal victory.

There *is* purpose in the struggle, even if we can't always see that in the present. My family and I attended the Hillsong Conference in Sydney, Australia recently, and during his message, pastor Steven Furtick said, "God speaks to our today from the vantage point of tomorrow." How great is that? God knows we get stuck in the mire and lose sight of His blessings, His purposes, and His goodness. Fortunately, God sees beyond our present darkness and trials; He sees our tomorrow, speaking to our present situation with His perspective that there is victory tomorrow.

Later, while commenting on Psalm 11, Wiersbe writes, "The Lord tests the righteous to bring out the best in them, but Satan tempts them to bring out the worst. When we trust the Lord in the difficulties of life, our trials work for us and not against us (2 Cor 4:7-18)."[20] I love that encouragement: while Satan will use trials to bring out the worst in people (think Job: Satan thought he would curse God if trials came), God uses those same trials to bring out the best in us, mold our character, draw us near to Him, and share His truth with the world. Though the process is challenging, we can't forget God is teaching us, growing us, and getting us in optimal shape for competition time.

CHOOSING TO FIND THE VICTORIES

When I was in high school, two teachers led a junior and senior girls' Bible study during lunch, and one day, one of the teachers spoke to us about thankfulness. She told us her freshman year of college was dismal. She had a difficult roommate, she knew she'd chosen the wrong college, her major was being eliminated, she was homesick, and a slew of other frustrating factors was thrown in there. Each morning she wrote down things she was thankful for, and on her very worst day, the only thing she came up with was that there were birds chirping outside, so clearly *they* must have been happy. Her only written praise that day read, "Thank You, Lord, for the birds chirping. At least they are happy." We laughed about the trials of college freshmen, but she told us even on those days, she was still able to find something to be grateful for—even if only the birds chirping by her window.

Just as we will probably have to make the daily choice for joy, we will probably also have to choose to find the victories amidst trials. They may not be readily apparent amidst cancer, treatment, side effects, and other struggles. However, if we'll take some time to look around and count our blessings, I think we'll find God is using us in great ways and that He is, in fact, giving us victories even during challenges.

In John 16:20, Jesus promises the disciples their grief will turn to joy. He doesn't say He'll *switch* their grief out for joy, but rather, when He predicts His upcoming death, Jesus explains: "I tell you the truth, you will weep and mourn while the world rejoices. You will grieve, but your grief will turn to joy." I think we have to adjust our perspectives on what victories and joy mean. We can't expect our trial to just vanish, finding a victory in its place; on the contrary, we need to expect that God can and will use this very trial as a victory in our lives.

Years ago, Rick Warren was interviewed on the success of his book *The Purpose-Driven Life*. I love what Warren said, especially about adjusting our perspective of life's good and bad days:

> Life is a series of problems: either you are in one now, you're just coming out of one or you're getting ready to go into another one. The reason for this is that God is more interested in your character than your comfort. God is more interested in making your life holy than He is in making your life happy. We can be reasonably happy here on earth, but that's not the goal of life. The goal is to grow in character, in Christlikeness.
>
> This past year has been the greatest year of my life—but also the toughest, with my wife, Kay, getting cancer. I used to think that life was hills and valleys—you go through a dark time, then you go to the mountaintop, back and forth. I don't believe that anymore. Rather than life being hills and valleys, I believe that it's kind of like two rails on a railroad track, and at all times you have something good and something bad in your life. No matter how good things are in your life, there is always something bad that needs to be worked on. And no matter how bad things are in your life, there is always something good you can thank God for. You can focus on your purposes, or you can focus on your problems.[21]

I've found his observations to ring very true in my life. Even during my freshman year of college when I loved life, I had to work through relationship issues and struggled in a couple of my classes. And, even during my senior year of college when I had cancer, I still had so many things to thank the Lord for. Just as we have to choose joy, I think if we can remember that, no matter how bad life seems to be, God is still good, He has blessed us with victories, and it's not all about us anyway, life will make a whole lot more sense.

PROCLAIMING THE VICTORIES

After we recognize our victories, we need to proclaim them. We have to share our stories because ultimately, they are God's stories and a testimony to Him. Ever noticed how many psalmists say things like, "I will tell of Your wonders" or "I have heard of Your wonders" (Ps. 9:1, 40:5, 78:4, 89:5, 105:5, 119:27, 136:4)? I tend to think, *Okay, that's nice, but God hasn't done any wonders in my life. I haven't seen any miraculous signs like water pouring from a rock or a pillar of fire leading me like those Old Testament guys did.* However, my Bible commentary clarifies that the word "wonders" refers to: "God's saving acts, sometimes involving miracles—as in the Exodus from Egypt, the desert wanderings, and the entrance into the promised land—and sometimes not, but *always involving the manifestation of God's sovereign lordship over events*" (emphasis mine).[22]

Have I seen the manifestation of God's sovereign lordship over events in my life? Absolutely. By that revised definition, God has done countless wonders in my life, and my job is to tell of them. That's a much simpler and more accessible command than I previously thought when I figured I could fabricate some miraculous-sounding signs and wonders. If I simply share the great things He has done in my life and the times when He has so clearly worked, I am telling of His wonders. I've found being a little bit vulnerable in sharing about my cancer diagnosis has yielded great encouragement and conversation.

On my absolute worst days when I've fed the self-pity train and wondered what the heck I'm doing with my life and what the point is, remembering the many times David and the other psalmists say they will tell of the Lord's good works in their lives fills me with renewed purpose. There's a reason believers aren't taken up to heaven upon conversion; someone has to tell the next generation about the Lord and His great love, and we're told pretty clearly we are those "someones." To bring meaning to what otherwise can seem like a worthless and fruitless existence is a huge victory.

God's wonders in our lives are victories, and we have to remember that truth in days of darkness and of light. Theologian Charles Spurgeon once said, "We write sorrows in marble, and mercies in the sand."[23] Yep, I'm a sand writer. Guilty. I definitely tend to write my trials in the marble to stay there forever where I can bring them up, reminding God how hard my life is, while I trace my blessings in the sand only to be washed away by the continual ebb and flow of the waves, and I'm probably not alone. We have to recognize the victories God gives, thank Him, and etch them into the marble, so when the next trial comes, we will see them and remember that, just as He has given us victory many times before, so He will again.

In the Word:

- **Psalm 18:28** "You, O Lord, keep my lamp burning; my God turns my darkness into light."
- **Psalm 66:5-6, 9-12** "Come and see what God has done, how awesome His works in man's behalf! He turned the sea into dry land, they passed through the waters on foot—come, let us rejoice in Him.... He has preserved our lives and kept our feet from slipping. For You, O God, tested us; You refined us like silver. You brought us into prison and laid burdens on our backs. You let men ride over our heads; we went through fire and water, but You brought us to a place of abundance."
- **Psalm 73:16-17** "When I tried to understand all this, it was oppressive to me till I entered the sanctuary of God; then I understood their final destiny."
- **Romans 8:37** "No, in all these things we are more than conquerors through Him who loved us."
- **2 Corinthians 2:14** "But thanks be to God, who always leads us in triumphal procession in Christ and through us spreads everywhere the fragrance of the knowledge of Him."

Recommended Reading:

- *The Hiding Place* retells author Corrie Ten Boom's experiences in a concentration camp. Though a heavy subject, her persistent hope, ability to see the silver lining in her trials, and sincere faith in God through immense difficulty are encouraging and uplifting.
- *Same Kind of Different as Me* by Ron Hall and Denver Moore is another empowering story of authentic faith amidst trials (warning, it's a tear-jerker, but it's moving and inspiring).

CHAPTER 9

Is it Over Yet?
Finishing Strong

Sunday, April 5, 2009

"Your path led through the sea, Your way through the mighty waters, though Your footsteps were not seen" (Psalm 77:19).

Wow, that verse pretty much sums up what I've been learning through reading *The Red Sea Rules*. What great imagery! The path often leads through the sea and mighty waters, but God brings us through both, though we don't always see His footprints next to us as we might like.

First, let me start with a low and go back to over a week ago (Friday, March 27th) when I underwent some scans at Northwestern. I started out at 8 a.m. with a Pulmonary Function test, moved to a MUGA scan for my heart at 9:15 a.m., and finished up with a CT scan at noon. At my eighth chemo treatment on March 18th, my nurse Michelle was having a hard time finding a vein (they're hiding, I believe, because they know what's coming). We realized I hadn't had much water, and dehydration makes it harder to find veins anyway. So, I've been trying to drink more water, but when it came time for these tests, I couldn't eat or drink anything twelve hours ahead of time, so my lack of hydration plus the fact that my veins hate needles contributed to lots of nurses poking my skin to try and find good veins.

For the MUGA and CT scans, each injection or IV took at least fifteen minutes and three pokes to find a working vein. With the MUGA scan, some saline seeped out of the vein, so a less-than-awesome bubble formed under the skin in my left hand. Then, for the CT scan, the nurse inserted contrast into a pretty small vein in my other hand, so I felt like I was getting stung by a bee for two minutes. When he offered to slow it down, my hand still hurt, so I told him I'd rather just go fast and get it over with than drag out the pain. To top off my Alexander-like "terrible, horrible, no good, very bad day,"[24] I had to drink nasty barium sulfate for the CT scan, which I downed by holding my nose and chugging.

When I got in my car to drive back to Wheaton, I'd *had* it. I was sick of being poked, having ugly bruises from all those pokes, and feeling cruelly used, like a lab rat. I had a short teary-eyed moment while driving away from the hospital, which I think has been one of the only mini-meltdowns I've had in this journey. You'd think I would lose it after chemo, but no; apparently the tests did it for me. I was sick and tired of it all.

My thoughts on the drive back ran something like this: I can look back on most struggles in my life and see that God has used each of those to strengthen and grow me, preparing me to go through the next trial. And I *know* that—God is faithful in using each struggle to draw me to Him and prepare me for whatever else He has for me. But then, I started asking, *Oh Lord, is this as hard as it gets? Because if this is all preparing me for something worse in the future, then that sucks and I'm not sure I can deal with that.*

While I know I'm lucky since life could be much worse, I just felt low. I realize we don't go through something difficult and then God says, "Ok, you've paid your dues. It's all smooth sailing from here," and I don't expect that. But, those were my thoughts, so I would love prayers to persevere but also to keep growing and learning what He has for me, as well as to keep trusting in His sovereignty. Thank you from the bottom of my heart for your prayers. I pray you will be blessed this week and that Easter will be such a great one this year—not just blending in with all the other celebrations you've had, but that Christ's sacrifice would really make an impact!

On Christ the solid Rock I stand,

Hannah
Posted at 2:08 p.m.

CRY

On the evening of all of those tests after my eighth treatment, as I drove away from the hospital, I was stuck in Chicago's rush hour traffic which was the cherry on top of my ever-worsening day. I turned on my car stereo, and Kelly Clarkson's (then) new CD started playing a song called "Cry." Though the song is about the carnage wrought by a broken relationship, it nevertheless captured so greatly how I felt: "Is it over yet? Can I open my eyes? Is this as hard as it gets? Is this what it feels like to really cry?"

"Hindsight's 20/20," my dad always reminds me. Take, for instance, the six months leading up to my diagnosis. The struggles I had as a counselor at Kanakuk, learning that leadership is so much more than being the loudest or doing everything, prepared me for a rough season of volleyball in which I was the captain of my team. Additionally, all of the frustrating injuries I'd had in volleyball where I felt like I couldn't catch a break taught me that asking the "Why?" question is not particularly helpful. My most recent knee injury a month before my cancer diagnosis reminded me of that and made me see the goal ahead was most important: playing for the final two weeks of my senior season and volleyball career. So I sucked it up, putting mind over matter. I can see how those injuries prepared me physically and mentally for my diagnosis of lymphoma one month later when I realized early on that whining or wasting time asking "Why?" would once again be ineffective when the end goal of remission (a.k.a. staying alive) was most important.

If all of those and other previous trials had prepared me for the next difficulty, then what on earth was *cancer* preparing me for? Though I knew each trial had made me who I was and strengthened me, amidst my tears I really wasn't sure if I wanted any part of that. On the other hand, I knew God doesn't give us the hardest trial we can face and then say, "Ok, you've served your time and had the worst. You're done. Have fun in life." I knew life after cancer wouldn't suddenly be immune to problems because I'd already suffered the worst I would face.

Still, I felt like crying out, "Lord, is it over yet? Is this as hard as it gets? Can I open my eyes yet?" The idea that my bout with cancer might only be preparing me for something in the future was—and still is—scary. Here's the thing, though: God already knows what we're thinking and where our hearts are. So, I think it's okay to cry out and ask if the worst is over yet. David and the other psalmists sure did (see Psalms 4, 6, 13, 22, 38, 69, 77, 86, 88, 142, 143). However, though we should be honest with God, we can't wallow in self-pity or lose sight of the finish line.

FINISH STRONG

One of my mottos in life is "Finish strong," and I have a black silicone bracelet I often wear to reinforce the idea. I'm pretty awesome at starting projects—whether cleaning my room, committing to serve, or writing a book. I have energy, enthusiasm, and a clear vision for whatever I'm doing. However, I'm exponentially more terrible at finishing said projects. Usually around halfway or two thirds of the way through a task, my energy and enthusiasm wane and I start to lose sight of the goal. Typically that means I end up simply slinking across that metaphorical finish line. I hate that I do that.

One summer during staff training week at Kanakuk, one of the camp leaders spoke to the counselors about finishing strong. He asked us to imagine living our entire lives on fire for the Lord, following and serving Him wholeheartedly. But, in the final decade of life, we lose that wholehearted devotion for whatever reason—we're tired, we've lost sight of the purpose, we feel as if we've served our time, etc. What a terrible way to meet our Maker! What a waste that decade would be, and what a shame to live so faithfully only to end in mediocrity.

Think about Solomon. When crowned king after David's death, Solomon immediately set about building the Lord's temple. He dedicated it and worked with fervor, seeking God as his father David had. Solomon publicly praised God among his subjects and exhorted them to do the same. But as time passed, he struggled to finish strong:

> As Solomon grew old, his wives turned his heart after other gods, and his heart was not fully devoted to the Lord his God, as the heart of David his father had been. He followed Ashtoreth the goddess of the Sidonians, and Molech the detestable god of the Ammonites. So Solomon did evil in the eyes of the Lord; he did not follow the Lord completely, as David his father had done (I Kings 11:4-6).

Though his songs of praise and wise proverbs characterize the beginnings of his faith, Solomon's concluding ruminations on life in Ecclesiastes are more telling. He surmises, "Yet when I surveyed all that my hands had done and what I had toiled to achieve, everything was meaningless, a chasing after the wind; nothing was gained under the sun" (Ecclesiastes 2:11).

What a pity. Solomon, the wisest and richest of all men—to the point that kings and queens of other lands came to glean wisdom from him—the man who had a rich heritage of faith and a great start walking with the Lord, drifted away in his old age. People speak so highly of David, but they don't discuss Solomon very often. I don't think we quite know what to do with him. Do we use him as a caution, although he *was* semi-faithful? Do we use him as an example though he walked away? Maybe we should just sweep him under the rug.... We can talk about how important God's wisdom is, but we hesitate to point to Solomon because even with the wisdom of God, he isn't exactly a role model to follow. David has a place in the hall of fame of faith in Hebrews chapter eleven, but the writer omits Solomon.

The author of Hebrews writes,

> All these people were still living by faith when they died. They did not receive the things promised; they only saw them and welcomed them from a distance. And they admitted that they were aliens and strangers on earth. People who say such things show that they are looking for a country of their own. If they had been thinking of the country they had left, they would have had opportunity to return. Instead, they were longing for a better country—a heavenly one. Therefore God is not ashamed to be called their God, for He has prepared a city for them (Hebrews 11:13-16).

All the people listed in this chapter had something in common: an eternal perspective keeping them focused on the Lord, living every day for Him, and finishing strong until the day they died.

The speaker's talk on finishing strong and those examples immediately struck a chord with me. Knowing I struggle to finish as well as I begin, I needed to adopt this motto. Making a concerted effort to finish strong has made such a difference in my life. I don't always want to or naturally finish strong, but by repeating those words, I've often found new resolve to complete the work with excellence rather than simply getting through it.

Just as this motto has made me more focused and determined in life, it was especially important in my battle with cancer. Early on, my family and various hospital staff members had warned me that the great outpouring of love, sympathy, and gifts would probably taper off toward the middle of treatment when my situation wasn't fresh in people's minds. Though I would still be in the throes of treatment, life would go on for everyone else. That might be a warning worth heeding: in any trial, the outpouring of support and encouragement will likely wane over time. Knowing that, we can't become cynical and put up walls to protect ourselves; we should accept the help as a blessing, not becoming bitter when life moves on for others. We've all probably done that to someone else before, too. Still, it's helpful to anticipate the hurdles we'll face along the way.

On top of the caution that my struggle would increase as support tapered off, I anticipated that the end of my journey through cancer would probably be more challenging than the start, that things might just get harder before they got easier, and I was right. You see, at first, I knew the road would be long, so I knew what I was up against and braced myself, armed with scores of supporters. I faced the problem head-on, deciding there was no point wasting energy and tears about the inevitable. The halfway point through treatment was a huge milestone, too, and it was one I eagerly celebrated. However, around treatments nine, ten, and eleven, when the end seemed close but still so far away, as side effects built upon each other, and as I became restless for life to return to normal, I struggled much more to stay positive than when I started the journey. Toward the last third of treatment, my initial resolve slowly dissipated as I struggled with contentment, staying focused on the goal, and remembering God's faithfulness.

In *A Million Miles in a Thousand Years,* Donald Miller talks about how eagerly people begin their careers in life yet how quickly their enthusiasm wanes when stuck in the middle of the journey. He writes,

> I think this is when most people give up on their stories. They come out of college wanting to change the world, wanting to get married, wanting to have kids and change the way people buy office supplies. But they get into the middle and discover it was harder than they thought. They can't see the distant shore anymore, and they wonder if their paddling is moving them forward. None of the trees behind them are getting smaller and none of the trees ahead are getting bigger.... It's like this with every crossing, and with nearly every story too. You paddle until you no longer believe you can go any farther. And then suddenly, well after you thought it would happen, the other shore starts to grow, and it grows fast. The trees get

taller and you can make out the crags in the cliffs, and then
the shore reaches out to you, to welcome you home, almost
pulling your boat onto the sand.[25]

How perfect is that analogy? We begin so full of energy, but as we lose
sight of the start and can't yet glimpse the finish line, we lose our hope
and motivation. We wonder if we're really getting any closer or if we're
just uselessly wearing ourselves out. But the thing is, if we can just press
on, once we see the other shore, the end will come so quickly.

RUNNING THE RACE

After my first half marathon, I felt an incredible sense of accomplishment.
I ran in spite of the fact that my knees and I have a love-hate relationship,
my orthopedic doctor flat-out told me I was not built to run long distances,
and my journey has included passing out, physical therapy, and dropping
loads of money on race fees, running shoes, and rehab.

Though I'm really good at setting goals three months at a time, long-term
goals are my nemesis. I start out really well and full of energy, and then,
somewhere in the middle, I lose sight of my purpose, get discouraged, and
want to bail out. I've always known this about myself, but somehow I'm
still surprised when I start muddling through situations. I *know* I need
to finish strong, I *tell* myself to finish strong, and yet, the act of finishing
strong isn't exactly made easier by either of those actions.

Training was frustrating because I faithfully stuck to my plan, yet I
saw people who trained minimally and had done very little athletically
before pick up the idea of running a half marathon and execute it without
problems. How annoying. Sometimes when I trained and, late in my
run, my knees wouldn't bend well, I shouted, "Seriously, can't I just be
exempt from this?!?" Who I shouted at is up for debate—probably half at
my knees and half at God. I always hoped my neighbors weren't within
earshot or they'd think I'm that crazy girl who yells at herself. At those
points, my thoughts ran like so: *I've already had cancer, so can't I, like, get*

a pass on having atrocious knees? Haven't I kind of served my time with the whole "my-body-hates-me" thing?

Obviously I know the answers to those, and ultimately, my race was insignificant in the grand scheme of the world, but I realized the race was significantly symbolic in my life. My frustrations in running which caused me to shout out how angry I was at the obstacles in my way are symptomatic of a bigger frustration. Underneath it all, I don't really need to run successfully; when I plead with God to let me run without having issues, what I'm really pleading for is to know I can finish something I've started.

Training was mostly solitary, and while that might sound sad or lame, I needed to train alone. As important as community is, I needed to know I can see a goal, motivate myself to faithfully prepare for it, and complete it—not because my parents make me, not because a doctor tells me to, and not because school or work requires it, but simply because I decide to. So, while running a half marathon is no big deal to others, my first one was to me. Through it, I learned that when I take on a difficult task, I *can* actually finish strong.

Communication books explain confidence is knowing you have the ability to complete something successfully. So get this: confidence isn't even *having* the ability to complete something successfully; it's *believing* we can be successful. Think about those terrible singers who audition for *American Idol*. They're confident, not because they *can* sing well, but because they *believe* they can sing well. Confidence for my run meant knowing I could complete it successfully. That doesn't mean the elements wouldn't intervene or my kneecaps wouldn't dislocate, but I was confident because I knew I *could* run my half marathon successfully. Though long-term goals aren't my forte, running showed me that I can successfully tackle them. I *can* finish strong. Sometimes we need that reminder, that confidence boost. We can finish strong.

THE RACE MARKED OUT FOR US

While we're on the topic of running as a metaphor for life, let's continue. Everyone is physically built for different tasks and athletic pursuits. For instance, Texas will become its own country again before I run a full marathon. The pain of cramping, hours of training, physical stamina, and mental endurance aren't my problems. If my knees stop bending at thirteen miles, I can't even imagine what would happen if I tried to run thirteen additional miles. Would they eventually go numb? Would my knees just...break? I'm not sure. So, I'll keep my gaze on half marathons, and while it's disappointing that I probably won't ever run a full marathon, I just wasn't made for that, so I'm over it. To others, running to the end of the street might seem loathsome, but where they excel at yoga or Pilates, I happily accept that my near-total lack of balance means I will never master the Firefly Pose.

Similarly, we all have different courses God has appointed for us. The author of Hebrews affirms this fact: "Therefore, since we are surrounded by such a great cloud of witnesses, let us throw off everything that hinders and the sin that so easily entangles, and let us run with perseverance the race marked out for us" (12:1). Breaking that down yields many spiritual truths. First of all, since we have so many amazing predecessors and fellow believers to support and encourage us, we need to press on. So many people have faced trials and walked through fires before us, and God will be faithful to us as we walk with Him just as He has throughout history.

Secondly, we have to throw off all hindrances, including sins of indulging in self-pity or bitterness at our condition. Running dehydrated *will* lead to my passing out (a truth I learned the hard way with one hundred yards to go in a 10K race). Because I know that now, I'm neurotic about hydrating before a run since I don't need an extra variable added to the already taxing exercise of running. Likewise, in order to press on and finish strong through trials, we can't get sidetracked by sin. Life is already hard enough, and cancer and our difficult situations only add to the challenge. We can't lose sight of the ultimate goal: finishing the race strong as God has called us to. We need to recognize our propensity to whine, doubt, or go through the motions and commit to avoiding those hindrances at all costs.

Additionally, we have to run with perseverance. If we're going to finish a long, taxing trial, we have to pray for perseverance. There's a point where we simply cannot do things on our own any longer. Luckily, God will supply our needs and help us continue on in the fight when we reach that point.

Finally, I love that the author of Hebrews calls life, "the race marked out for us." Physically, a marathon isn't in the cards for me. Metaphorically, my race isn't over (as evidenced by the fact that I'm currently writing this). God has marked out a specific purpose and time for each of our lives. We are on this earth just briefly but for an appointed amount of time. That time is going to include various joys and trials. The race marked out for me included cancer, and God gave me the perseverance to run that leg of the race. I'm sure there will be many more legs of the race to come, and I know He will provide for those as well.

Jesus lived on this earth for a mere thirty-three years. Though Christ ministered to people daily as He grew up (see Luke 2), His official public ministry lasted for three years. Was His life a failure because it was cut short? Yeah, that's probably a dumb question. And the thing is, His life *wasn't* cut short. God had appointed that specific time for Him on earth, and in that time, Jesus changed eternity.

My friend Liz's mom passed away from pancreatic cancer when we were in high school. At her funeral, I was deeply moved and inspired. Mrs. Allbright lived a full life, serving people in any and every way she could. I love the verse her pastor used to memorialize her life. In 2 Timothy 4:7, the apostle Paul says, "I have fought the good fight, I have finished the race, I have kept the faith." I learned that verse in school for our third grade music production, but it didn't click until Mrs. Allbright's funeral.

She epitomized those words, faithfully serving the Lord every day of her life until her very last breath. She fought the good fight, she finished the race set out for her, and she kept the faith. She finished strong.

I would love for that verse to describe my life: I've fought courageously, completed the race marked out for me, and all along kept the faith. Paul knew he was near his end when he wrote 2 Timothy, and though I doubt he was looking forward to how things would play out, he was confident he had finished strong. He knew he would successfully follow the Lord through the end because he didn't rely on his own strength.

More than any other lesson I've encountered about finishing strong, the greatest truth has been that, when I can't find the strength within myself or when the future ahead looks bleak and I have no idea what it holds, if I'll rely on God, He will meet me at my point of need, carrying me through to the finish line. We need to finish strong the race marked out for us.

THE OTHER SHORE

Psalm 77:19-20a affirms the secret to finishing strong: "Your path led through the sea, Your way through the mighty waters, though Your footsteps were not seen. You led Your people like a flock." God leads us though we don't always see His footsteps along the way. When the path gets dark and we can only see one step ahead, God will lead us on.

My way through cancer became pretty dark toward the end. In case you thought this book was all a testimony to my upbeat, can-do attitude, maybe you'll finally believe I'm a cynic. I was upbeat when I had to be, but toward the end, I "went into my dark place" as we like to say in my family. All of my friends discussed their post-graduation plans—from their jobs to their weddings to where they were moving—but when others asked me about my plans, I wanted to shout, *Um, I'm trying to stay alive, here, so thanks for asking!* In fact, I may have actually said that out loud to a few inquisitive people with unfortunate timing.

I struggled through treatments nine, ten, and eleven, frustrated that the course wasn't over yet, disheartened, and pleading for God to move. My physical pain mounted as time passed. Days five and six grew progressively worse as treatment wore on, and though I didn't initially have bad nausea after chemo, after treatment eleven, I threw up most mornings.

In addition, my blood counts continued deteriorating, and after my eleventh treatment, I had to give myself a shot to temporarily boost my while blood cells. Dr. Gordon and Michelle warned that it would cause my cells to expand in my bone marrow, so I might feel pretty strong pain in my long bones, or my legs and hips, within a couple days. I gave myself the shot, but after forty-eight hours, I hadn't experienced any pain yet. Apparently medicine takes time to affect me and balks at predictions because, like my experience with chemo's side effects, the pain came two days later, when I least expected it.

On the night before my final college exam, I experienced the worst pain I've ever had in my life. My back was filled with searing pain. I can't even explain how much it hurt except to say that for some reason I started laughing. I realize I sound crazy because normal people don't laugh at excruciating pain, but I think I maxed out the "rate your pain" scale and added a new category: pain to the point of delirious laughter. Dr. Gordon prescribed Vicodin for such an occasion, but since the effects hit later than expected, I found myself in pain beyond speech and tears on the night before my exam. There was no way I could miss the 8 a.m. test the next morning, and without enough time for the Vicodin's sleep-inducing effects to wear off, I could only take some Tylenol, pray relentlessly for peace, and hope to fall asleep. The next morning, I raced through my exam, finishing it as quickly as possible since I was still on the verge of screaming.

Mentally and emotionally, my struggle intensified as well. Though I was so close to the finish line—just ten days away from my final treatment and a few weeks after that until I felt better each day—I couldn't believe how impossibly far away the end seemed.

A few days later, my parents, sisters, and grandparents flew up for graduation, and I was so thankful to sit through the ceremony, walk across the stage—wig and all—and receive my diploma. That day was one of the proudest of my life, and it provided a temporary respite from my internal battle to finish strong. However, the next morning, my family left to go back home and to work, I returned to my house exhausted, and my friends started packing up and moving on to new adventures. I stayed behind, feeling alone and pretty sorry for myself as I faced a still murky future. Even though I would pack up and move home a week later, I couldn't move on to the next phase in life until I was certain I'd make it through the present one.

Spiritually, I needed God to help me out, too. All throughout the journey I prayed for God to sustain me, but in the last six weeks of treatment, I daily begged for God's presence. I was genuinely grateful for graduating and all God had blessed me with, but I was losing heart and hope. I was at the end of my rope, and without others around to encourage me anymore, I felt alone and in desperate need for God to sustain me. Overall, I'd definitely say I hit my low point.

Then, suddenly, May 14th, my final day of treatment, arrived. As I stepped out of the elevator onto the twenty-first floor for chemo number twelve, somehow my weeks of desperately trying to look beyond the clouds ended as the light started to break through. This was it; the end of the challenge was near. I found, just as Miller asserted, that suddenly I'd arrived at that other shore. Before I knew it, my final treatment ended and I could go home. I left the cancer center and walked to the car in a daze. Soon I was sitting in the car, heading away from the hospital, and breathing a deep sigh of relief. I knew days five and six still lurked around the corner, I had months to years of side effects still to manage, and I wasn't completely out of the danger zone for a recurrence, but I also knew the worst was over and I'd made it solely because God carried me through the long night.

I realized that, though I'd been frustrated and feeling like it was time for God to show up again, He'd been there all along, carrying my ever-weakening body and spirit along. I felt His comfort more during my final treatment than during any of the previous eleven when I was more upbeat and encouraged by others. When I came to the end of my ability to finish strong and had exhausted the support from others to help me get there, God held me together just when I wondered how I'd make it. I've found He does that a lot—He holds us together and leads us through the darkness right when we falter and can't seem to take another step. When we come to the end of ourselves, the Lord leads us on, helping us finish strong with His calling though we may never see His footsteps along the way.

In the Word:

- **Psalm 48:14** "For this God is our God for ever and ever; He will be our guide even to the end."
- **Psalm 49:15** "But God will redeem my life from the grave; He will surely take me to Himself."
- **Psalm 71:14-15, 20-21** "But as for me, I will always have hope; I will praise You more and more. My mouth will tell of Your righteousness, of Your salvation all day long, though I know not its measure....Though You have made me see troubles, many and bitter, You will restore my life again; from the depths of the earth You will again bring me up. You will increase my honor and comfort me once again."
- **Psalm 119:112** "My heart is set on keeping Your decrees to the very end."

On the Web:

- Finish Strong (www.finishstrong.com) is a pertinent website created by Dan Green who has also written a book on the subject. The company sells silicone wristbands, decals, books, media, and other merchandise.
- Nick Vujicic was born without limbs, and he travels the world sharing his testimony. Search "Nick Vujicic Finish Strong" to find videos in which he talks about getting back up and finishing strong.

CHAPTER 10

Where Do I Go From Here?

Tuesday, September 8, 2009

"But I trust in Your unfailing love; my heart rejoices in Your salvation. I will sing to the LORD, for He has been good to me" (Psalm 13:5-6).

Wow. Once again, it's been *way* too long. I've been meaning to update for a few weeks now, but things have been crazy, and time is *flying*. Literally. Ok, not literally, but it's gone by quickly.

Friday concluded our fifth week of school at Hawaii Baptist Academy (see what I mean?!?). We are now only three weeks away from Fall Break, which means three weeks until I get to see my family and friends back on the mainland. Don't get me wrong—Hawaii has been awesome, but it's definitely far from those I love and miss.

You're probably wondering how I'm doing health-wise. I am doing well! I still don't have all of my stamina back—I saw that last weekend when I surfed and almost cried when I had to swim for what seemed like forever with zero energy—but it's definitely coming. I'm working out with another teacher (we're taking a Zumba class!), and I'm enjoying being able to be active. I still have to sleep a good amount. Because I have to get up around 6 a.m. each day, I'm able to get around seven and a half hours of sleep, but I come home each day fully exhausted. Praise the Lord that I'm able to do this and teach though! My hair is growing back, slowwwwly, but still.... It'll be a while until I go wigless, and that's actually been frustrating. I don't know if I shared in my last blog, but I didn't foresee how long recovery would take. I think after all the treatments ended, this has been a harder ordeal than when I was actually going through chemo, which sounds crazy.

My mom and I were talking about this when she was here in Honolulu helping me move. I think during everything, we were just so focused on getting through it that that's all we did: get through it. It's been after the fact that I've had more thoughts of, *What was the point of that?* wondering what to do with the past year in my life. For my mom, too, it's been after the fact that all the events of the past year have really set in, and she said there was a moment recently when she began remembering everything and started crying, exhausted over all that happened.

I told a few friends it's hard to figure out what to do with the past year in a sense of, how do I still remember all the things God did while moving on and living life? I don't want to be *that* person who always sits back and says, "Wellllll, when I had *cancer,*" but I also don't want to move on and forget what just happened. It's been significant enough that I *know* God had a purpose in it, and I know it's impacted my life, but I can't tell you how necessarily. So the question remains: What to do with this past year?

It's getting time for me to turn in so I can teach my little students effectively in the morning. Basically, I am doing well—just trying to process. I know God is good and has a purpose for everything. I think I'm struggling with trusting where He'll lead me since I'm a little afraid that, if I've been there, done that with cancer, He might lead me somewhere else even harder in the future. I'd love prayers to rest in Him as I process and try to move on while remembering all the awesome things God taught me and incredible people He blessed me with. I'd also cherish your prayers for wisdom in teaching these kids—that they wouldn't learn just about public speaking or literature, but they would really and genuinely see God.

On Christ the solid Rock I stand,

Hannah
Posted at 3:42 a.m.

MOON WALKING AND CANCER

After all is said and done with the whole cancer process, I still have so much to learn.

One of the hardest and most unexpected struggles with cancer was what to do with it when the last treatment ended. Comedian Brian Regan does a bit called "I walked on the moon" where he talks about how people try to one-up each other in social situations. The gist of it is he tells a story at a dinner party trying to impress his peers, but after he finishes, a guy in the corner pipes up trying to top his story. Brian Regan laments the human condition of having to one-up each other, so he says he has a social fantasy in which he is one of the twelve astronauts who've been to the moon. He points out that they hold the ultimate trump card because they can beat anyone's story at any time. People can rave on and on about themselves and their accomplishments, but all the astronaut has to do is casually mention, "I walked on the moon," and the floor is automatically his.

In a way, cancer is similar. I've been in conversations in which people are talking about their struggles or injury stories, and friends of mine will sort of cast a knowing glance at me or bring up, "Hannah's a cancer survivor," and conversation automatically turns to me. As I started writing this book, I can't even tell you how many conversations went like this:

Stranger: "Nice to meet you. What do you do?"

Me:	"I took a year off of teaching to write a book, so I'm working retail part-time, substitute teaching, and coaching club volleyball."
Stranger:	"Wow, you're writing a book? That's awesome! What's it about?"
Me:	*Oh gosh, here we go...* "Thanks. Um, it's for young adults with cancer."
Stranger:	"Cancer? Do you have some experience with that?"
Me:	"Well..." (*insert hesitant pause before launching into a short summary*).

Sometimes I just say, "Yeah. Had cancer; everything's fine" in one breath to preempt the inevitable concern and follow-up questions.

"Cancer" has the power to both halt and begin conversations, and it's such a weighty word that if you just throw it around, people will inevitably want to know more. Anytime you mention having had chemo or a wig, you're opening your own Pandora's box filled with complicated stories, details, procedures, and emotions all involved within the simple word "cancer."

I knew I didn't want to be *that* person always referring back to, "Well, when I had *cancer...*" and living completely in the past. Yet, it was too big, too monumental in my life to move on and forget it as if nothing had even happened. Something *had* happened and changed me, but I couldn't bring it up every minute of every day. I was so much more than a cancer survivor. While it was definitely a huge part of life, it didn't encapsulate all of who I was and the work God had done in me. I didn't want to draw attention to myself or hijack all conversation, but how could I keep from avoiding that time in my life altogether?

It's been said Neil Armstrong was chosen as the first person to walk on the moon in part because he commanded the mission but mostly because he didn't have a big ego. NASA thought he could handle the honor without gloating about it.[26] Armstrong retired from NASA shortly after walking on the moon, and though he didn't completely avoid the subject, he managed to keep a semi-low profile living in Ohio, staying out of politics, and choosing to teach in smaller colleges.

I'd like to think Neil Armstrong might have dealt with very similar questions to what I (and countless others) faced post-cancer. How does an astronaut never bring up the fact that he walked on the moon so as not to steal the floor or sound arrogant when, in reality, it's a *big* deal and a huge part of his life? Cancer and walking on the moon are completely different scenarios, but both alter a person's future. Though I didn't worry about retiring and avoiding the national spotlight, I struggled with what to do with the experience. It was too hard to separate myself from the memories, people, and events intertwined with cancer to never bring up the subject in everyday life.

A PROBLEM OF PERSPECTIVE

I found that the problem of fitting cancer into everyday life is similar to what occurs after a mission trip. If you've ever been on one, people will talk about avoiding spiritual highs and how it's so hard to stay at that place when you get home. That's definitely true and something difficult to deal with. But, rather than a spiritual high after my trips to the Dominican Republic and other countries, the problem I faced was something different. I struggled, not to stay close to the Lord, but more with the problem of perspective. When you go on a trip like that, you see things—maybe God at work, maybe the bigger picture, maybe things that challenge your priorities or the world as you knew it—and all these things broaden your perspective.

The hardest thing for me was seeing from a totally new perspective only to return home to my everyday world where I had school and couldn't build houses to shelter orphans all day. How do you make sense of all you saw in the other world, reconciling that new perspective with your everyday world? All at once, everything has shifted in you though the world around you may look very much the same.

Similarly, my biggest struggle post-treatment was how to make sense of all that had occurred the previous year, reconciling it with everyday life. After chemo and graduation, I moved home to Dallas for the summer, only to get a teaching job in Honolulu for which I had to repack all my stuff, ship it across the ocean, and move by mid-July. Once I arrived, things moved quickly, and I settled into a regular schedule of teaching, starting to work out again, grading papers, and setting goals for my life three months at a time. Being around new people, none of whom had actually walked through the previous year with me—the most influential thing I'd ever been through—was difficult. Anything people knew about that year was from what I'd told them; none of them had actually *lived* it with me. To them, those were just stories from my past, as if I was sharing about my high school sports career or showing them a picture of my friends on the mainland they'd never met and that had no context.

To others, my experience with cancer was an episode. But to me, it was an epic.

This problem of perspective continued as I struggled to reconcile such a huge event in my life with the present: a very regular schedule where things slowly fell into a routine and, but for my short hair, most other side effects eventually healed and disappeared. How was I to reconcile going through something where my whole perspective had changed? I now cared deeply about cancer and those going through it; I grew impatient with smokers and tanners who, it seemed, brought such horror on themselves; after all the incredible ways people had blessed me, my relationships had taken on a new intensity. How was I supposed to return to the normalcy of life before the big "C word" entered once my whole perspective had changed? How was I supposed to move on to quiet living, no longer flooded with emails and hugs, people daily reassuring me they were with me, and being surrounded by so much support?

I like to think time after cancer was like the sixteenth minute when my fifteen minutes of fame ended. Realistically, I was important and at the forefront of people's thoughts during treatment. Maybe it's not always how I wanted them to be thinking of me—with pity or sorrow over my condition—but I was still on their minds. Once treatment ended, though, life went on. People moved on (as they should have). However, I was still left with the aftermath: some lingering side effects like half-attached toenails; veins that, courtesy of chemo, look like I should attend Narcotics Anonymous; hair that took a *long* time to grow back (though to everyone else, it seemed so fast). I was left with all this and more. I wondered how to make sense of the experience and especially how to reconcile this new perspective with the ordinary world. While life seemed to be back to normal, it had all changed for me—not physically, but in what I'd seen and been through.

THE NEW "NORMAL"

Life seemed to be without trials for a while after finishing chemo. After such a tumultuous year, I struggled with life's normal routine. Though I longed for life to return to normal during chemo, afterward, it was so hard to go back to the mundane where (thankfully!) I didn't worry about grave things like my blood counts, pacing myself, and whether the cancer was going away or not. Instead, I had to worry about grading papers, figuring out how to teach, and making sure I stayed in touch with friends—not the same weight at all.

Two months into the school year, I met with a group of female teachers during lunch one day, and we talked through prayer requests. I told them I was loving my job, living in Hawaii, and the other teachers. But I had this feeling of just waiting for something bad to happen, as if it was all too good to be true. Things in life don't typically go as I plan (case in point: cancer). Since I wanted the job in Hawaii and got it—though initially I was turned down—it almost felt too good to be true. I had this unnerving fear that any day I would get a call from my parents saying there'd been an accident or something for which I'd have to leave Hawaii and move home. In fact, one night I dreamed that my parents died on a trip, and I woke up going through the scenario, wondering what I'd do, and committing to pack up and move home to take care of my sister so she could finish high school living in our house rather than with relatives. Yes, I was paranoid that night. But if not something tragic like that, I figured it was only a matter of time until my dream job soured and the charm of it all somehow ended.

I realized that when times are going well, I'm sitting on edge, waiting for something bad to break the magic of it all. With a rough year and a half behind me, I came to the point where I expected struggles and hardships as the norm. We *are* warned throughout the New Testament that the road of faith won't be an easy one; in fact, at times, we're promised we will face suffering and trials, and James even exhorts us to consider it pure joy when we *do* face trials (James 1:2). However, my post-cancer apprehension that because things were going well, something terrible was bound to happen, wasn't me being watchful and warned. I was paranoid and erroneously thinking something was out to get me and spoil anything good in life.

All of these thoughts revealed something about me (other than my hyper-vigilant and irrational train of thought): I subconsciously believed things were too good to last. Ultimately, this belief meant that at some level, I thought God was not good. I never would have said that out loud, and I didn't think He was the Grinch out to steal my Christmas, but to some degree, I thought He wouldn't let the blessings linger for long. When I came to that realization, I was appalled at my lack of faith in God's goodness after all He'd done for me and *especially* in light of the previous year. I was just like the Israelites who, having seen God miraculously part the Red Sea, go back to grumbling, not trusting God, and doubting His goodness and plan. I sat and wondered how I could question His goodness when He'd just cured me of cancer. *Really, Hannah?* I said to myself, *He can walk me through cancer, and then I somehow doubt His goodness? Who does that, and what is wrong with me?!?*

GOD IS GOOD

Glad to have finally confronted my underlying fears, I remembered God actually *loves* us. Yes, we all know that and can say it and sing the song, but do we really believe it? God is not out to get us, something I subconsciously feared. If He is, why would He send His only Son to die for us, the sinful, often faithless, and insignificant people we are? No, in all of His dealings with His people and in my life, too, love is the motivation—sometimes tough love, but love nonetheless.

God is not some callous deity sitting up there in heaven looking down on us like a nineteenth century European monarch. It's not like He says, "Hmm...you know, things have been going well too long for Hannah. The peasant needs to suffer. Looks like it's time for a humbling!" (I picture Oprah saying this during one of her "Favorite Things" episodes: "Everyone gets a *humbling!*"). Yes, there are times when we have to learn hard lessons and face trials, being humbled in the process. But knowing that the God who loves us and is *good* is in control should provide solace in those times. Remembering His character is crucial. I've learned to think His attitude isn't, "Time for a trial but you'll learn and grow, so suck it up," but rather one of hurting with us as we hurt, walking through each trial with us, and knowing, much as a parent must, that though this pains and grieves everyone involved, we *will* be better for it.

One of my greatest memories of chapel at Wheaton was one in which the speaker talked about what lies beyond the printed words on the pages of the Bible. I can't tell you who was speaking, and I don't remember all of the references, but I do remember him highlighting Job. We know the story: God and Satan meet up, a challenge ensues, tragedy strikes, and Job won't curse God but eventually cries out "Why?" God finally steps in and puts him in his place, and Job shuts up. Who are we to question God? Were we there? Did we order all of creation? I don't *think* so! So, shut up. Stop whining. End of story. Dumb humans. Right?

Wrong.

That's how I used to view it. This speaker, however, pointed out there is a context to written word, an emotion not present in printed text but underlying the words—a fact I should have realized as a literature major. Tone matters. Now, I was not there when all the events of Job occurred, I did not hear God speak these words, and I don't pretend to fully know the mind of God, so this is conjecture. However, let's think about the character of God. He is all-knowing: He knew what was going on when Job didn't. He is all-powerful: He was still in control and seated on His throne though Job's life seemed out of control and upside down. He is faithful: He protected Job and later blessed him beyond his previous status. And, He is *good*, not callous: He wasn't doing these things just for kicks or a petty power struggle with the devil.

With that in mind, I tend to think the conversation with Job went less with attitude or God smack-talking Job. *I* would say, "Oh, no. You did *not!*" and then haughtily put someone in his or her place. Thankfully, God is not like us. We have to consider His attributes when He asks those questions: Were we there? Can we know all? Did we create all? If we remember His character, I think we'll see that as our Father, God spoke them more gently and filled with love than if we said those same words. Is He stern at times? Yes. However, God isn't full of attitude and pride.

So, was I there? No, I can honestly admit I wasn't there when God created all, ordered the universe, and still faithfully fulfills His promises today. Do I go crawl in a hole now because God won the argument and I have no way to respond to those rhetorical questions? No. As He reminds me that *I* wasn't there but He *was*, I shouldn't feel like a worm but rather realize I don't know all, but He does, and I can rejoice in the fact that He's in control though I'm a total mess.

I DON'T UNDERSTAND

One of the more profound things I have unwittingly cried out to God is that I don't understand. Robin, my teammate's mom who shaved my head, was diagnosed with breast cancer in March of 2010, ten months after my final chemo treatment. Our paths intersected one day on the island of Kauai as their family arrived for spring break and my vacation there ended. They were such a dear and faithful family who had loved me and served me greatly in my time of need, so I felt burdened for them when I saw them that night. After we all went to dinner, I headed out and sat on the beach in front of our hotel where I started to journal and pray about my frustration and hurt for them. Looking at the vastness of the ocean waves and the clouds passing by the starry and moon-lit sky, I cried out in frustration through my tears, "I don't understand!" As I tried to process, I shortly realized I was right: I legitimately *don't* understand.

Like Job, I don't understand what God is doing. I don't know why such a godly woman would have to be diagnosed with breast cancer; I don't know why my sweet teammate Kaitlyn, who had just finished dealing with her teammate's cancer, had to then see her own mom face cancer; I don't know why that family—or any family—has to go through things like cancer. And honestly, there are still times today when I don't know why I had to go through cancer either. I can't see God's plan and reasons, and yet, I know He *has* them, and He is faithful and good. My tears went from frustration to acceptance that night as I realized how true my words were, and I repeated my cry that I simply didn't understand.

That same phrase uttered with a clearer perspective has greatly helped me to process and reconcile this new perspective with the old everyday routine of life. I *don't* understand what God was doing, what He wants to do with my lymphoma, how He wants to use me, and on a grander scale, why there is so much pain in this world. And, though God helps me understand these things a little better over time as I grow with Him, I can admit my ignorance freely, knowing that while I *don't* understand, God *does*.

SEASONS

Another of my favorite worship songs is "Blessed be Your Name" by Matt Redman. I've always loved the lyrics: "Every blessing You pour out I'll turn back to praise. And when the darkness closes in, Lord, still I will say: 'Blessed be the name of the Lord, blessed be Your name.'" Additionally, the lyrics from the end of the song have helped me through difficult times. They say, "You give and take away; You give and take away. My heart will choose to say, 'Lord, blessed be Your name.'"[27] In struggles, these words have proven again and again to be such a great anthem to proclaim. Despite the situation, my heart will make the choice to keep trusting Him. They come from Job and tie in to when he surmises to his wife, "Can we accept just the good from God and not the bad, too?" which is an important reminder (Job 1:21; 2:10). We expect everything to be perfect, and when something comes to upset our equilibrium, we cry out, "But *why?*" forgetting that the good times were blessings and not the norm.

While I always connected with those lyrics during hard times, I learned post-cancer that those words are also relevant in the good times. It's been hard to simply accept His blessings and *rest* in them, trusting He is good and remembering He wants the best for us. When painful things happen, God is no less good or on our side. In good times, I have to *also* remember God is good and not out to get me. I can't be waiting for something bad to happen as if God wants to rain on my parade.

That brings me back to the song. The lyrics I love explain that in bad times, we have to choose to say, "Lord, blessed be Your name." However, the words also remind us, "Every *blessing* You pour out, I'll turn back to praise." Even in times of blessing, we need to cry out to the Lord and give Him praise. God gives and takes away, and while I typically focus on crying out and bringing Him praise in the hard times, I also need to remember that He *gives!* And when He gives, my heart will *also* choose to say, "Lord, blessed be Your name."

Sometimes people talk about how it can be harder to trust God in easier times because we forget our need, and I've definitely struggled with that. But more than trusting in Him in the easy times, we need to accept *every* season in our lives since He is over them all. If that season is a particularly hard one, we have to cling to Him, trusting He will bring us through just as He did with the Israelites and the Red Sea. If that season is filled with blessings, we have to cling to Him, not feeling guilty for the blessing (since it's not ours to determine anyway) and not anxiously fearing the next trial or hard time, as if God is some spiteful person eagerly anticipating the next chance to humble us through a hard lesson.

In hard times, God is good! In easy times, God is good! In all times, God is good! We may not always like our circumstances, and we may struggle with trusting in every season, but God is still *God* and still *good* in all of them. He wants the best for us, and while sometimes that means we have to learn hard lessons, in others He blesses us with the desires of our hearts.

GREAT IS THY FAITHFULNESS

At my roommate Kelli's wedding not too long ago, the congregation sang "Great is Thy Faithfulness." Many college friends, including my teammates Stef, Kelli, and other girls who'd taken care of me during chemo, were there. I guess being surrounded by them and singing the words to that hymn all of a sudden became too much for me. As we sang, "Morning by morning new mercies I see. All I have needed Thy hands hath provided, great is Thy faithfulness Lord unto me," I was touched by how true those statements have been in my life. The fact that I wake up each day shows me God's new mercies every morning.

When we reached the second verse, I lost it. As we sang, "Strength for today and bright hope for tomorrow," tears started pouring from my eyes. I couldn't stop them. I kept thinking, *Get it together, Hannah!* One of the girls leaned over and asked if I was okay. I think she figured I was so deeply moved by the wedding ceremony, but since I'm not overly sentimental, that wasn't the case—though I wish for the happy couple's sake it was. I was overwhelmed by God's goodness in *my* life and how so many of these friends around me had helped me in that impactful time. Even more, I was struck by what a perfect line that was in such a difficult time in my life.

Never before had I so physically relied on Him to get me through each day. Though emotional struggles are deeply trying, there's something about having to *literally* use God's strength that affected me in a new and real way. He truly was my strength for each day, and as I sit here having made it through the storm of cancer, He was and is my bright hope for tomorrow.

In sixth grade, my class memorized Jeremiah 29:11, and the oft-quoted verse has stuck with me: "'For I know the plans I have for you,' declares the Lord, 'plans to prosper you and not to harm you, plans to give you hope and a future.'" That future might look different than how you or I might imagine. In fact, in my life, it pretty much always goes differently than how I imagine. However, His plan is to prosper us *in Him*. That was hard to fully embrace at times when I didn't exactly feel like "cancer" and "prosper" were synonymous, but we have to remember faith is "being sure of what we hope for and *certain of what we do not see*" (Hebrews 11:1). I'm choosing to have faith in His plan, and I'm certain that He is good.

Whether we have stage IV cancer, we've lost a loved one, or life seems pretty good, God has plans for our lives, and they are great. He is our bright hope for tomorrow, however long that tomorrow may be. We can't doubt He is using trials to significantly impact our own lives and the lives of others. We need to rest in the fact that we can't always see what He's doing, but we know He is faithful and has perfect plans. When we struggle to figure out what the heck to do with a crazy experience, we have to trust He is currently using us even as we confusedly try to reconcile our perspectives with experiences. Remember, God is God and we aren't. We only see a fragmented part of the picture He's painting.

I SEE THE LIGHT

I love Disney. I have all my life: the music, the movies, the parks, the clever characters, the witty dialogue, Walt's vision and inspiration. Call me a nerd, but I love it all and have no shame about it. I saw the movie *Tangled* promptly upon its theatrical release and was enchanted by the lantern scene upon the lake as the characters sing "I See the Light." I loved the scene's stunning visual imagery and the song's perfect melody and harmony; it might be one of my favorite scenes from a movie.

When I heard there was a real-life lantern floating at the beach closest to my apartment in Honolulu, I put the event on my calendar in all caps and awaited the evening's arrival. When it came, I grabbed my camera and zoom lens and headed down to Ala Moana Beach Park. It was held on Memorial Day, and an estimated 40,000 people showed up to honor their loved ones who had passed away, to celebrate their lives, and to congregate together as three thousand lanterns floated out to sea.

Though my motives in attending the event were less than honorable since they were *Tangled*-inspired, when I met a woman who let me share her beach towel and told me she and her daughter had a lantern to honor her deceased husband, I was sobered by how meaningful this event was for so many people. When the time arrived for lighting the lanterns, volunteers helped people illuminate their lamps and gave instructions on when to release them. Since the lighting process took a while, I had ample time to look at the lanterns of those around me, and they brought tears to my eyes. Many people wrote notes on the sides of the lanterns, some to fallen soldiers from their wives and children, some to grandparents from their kids and grandkids, and others to friends and family members who had passed away. Seeing a child write, "Dear Dad, we all miss you a lot, but I miss you most of all" broke my heart.

My analysis of the event went through a few stages as I stood there. First, I saw that people need to hope there's something else out there after life on earth. A Buddhist priest welcomed everyone, a Catholic priest spoke at the beginning of the ceremony, and many people around me said they weren't "religious" at all. It was an odd collection of people who had very little going on with the Lord. However, they were still there to light lanterns, and I was saddened watching so many lost people who wouldn't admit their need for God but were still somehow hoping their deceased loved ones would get these paper lanterns somewhere "out there."

Next I saw that people have a need to commemorate those who have passed away and acknowledge their loss. Sometimes I think we're afraid their memory might get lost or the vision of them might become too blurred if we don't take time to honor and remember them. Those left behind need to commemorate those who've passed away so as to hang on to the memory that they were here, they lived, and they were loved.

When the bell rang signaling people to send off their lanterns, I was overwhelmed with how sad yet beautiful the scene was, and my analysis reached its next stage. As the lanterns floated out across the Hawaiian waters, I realized that for many, sending off a lantern was also a peaceful way for survivors and those left behind with loss to grieve and let go. For Christians in the crowd, I hope there was an understanding that no one was receiving those lanterns. It's like my mom always says when she discusses her funeral and burial. She forbids us to leave flowers on her grave or spend money on a nice casket or tombstone because, as she sees it, she won't be there, so we shouldn't waste our time or money.

I fully believe I won't be stuck in the ground when I die either. Praise the Lord for His redemption and for bringing us to Himself! However, I always tell her she's missing the point. Tombstones are really more of a way for the *survivors* to remember their loved ones, to cope, and hopefully to slowly let go of the pain of loss. I think that's how many saw those lanterns. They needed to be there not just for the sake of honoring their loved ones but especially so they could personally let go. Physically pushing off a lantern into the water was such a beautiful symbol of that process of pushing off and letting go, and I was moved.

Finally, after most people had let go of their lanterns and the tributes were peacefully floating out of the bay, I looked around at the huge crowd of people who had gathered, and I came to my final stage in analyzing the event. For the tens of thousands who gathered at Ala Moana Beach Park that night, there was something important about standing with others who were also experiencing pain and loss. Without even knowing each other's stories, people had a communal sense of closure and healing, unified by their suffering.

Though I at first thought it was sad and kind of pointless for people to send out letters on lanterns hoping their loved ones would receive them, I left the event with the realization that people needed to write those letters on the lanterns not so much for the lost ones but rather for their own sakes, as a way to commemorate, heal, and let go. Furthermore, for so many people to convey deeply personal hurt in such a public atmosphere, people must have a need to hurt together and recognize each other's pain. It doesn't matter if everyone standing there knew their neighbors' stories or not; it was simply enough that they were there, and that created a bond.

BUILDING AN ALTAR

How does lantern floating relate to where we go from our trials? When you have cancer, you become part of a club you never wanted to be in. Though so many can't—and never will—fully understand what I went through, I've found so many others have been there, and even if they had a different kind of cancer thirty years earlier, they understand and can relate. That communal sense of struggle and loss can help with healing.

In addition, I needed to find a way to commemorate the pain, loss, and experience of cancer, as we all need to after trials. If you want to craft a lantern and float it in your pool, that's great, but if not, find a way to mark the event as if to say, "I won't forget all God has done in my life and in this time." Conveniently, I've got my own visual reminder of my experience on my left bicep.

During one of my check-ups midway through chemo, one of the nurses ran out of the regular tape the hospital uses, so she used some lame excuse for tape made of satin that she found to keep a cotton ball in place over my IV wound. When I took the tape off later and noticed red spots, I assumed they indicated the satin tape had been too tight or something and they would fade. Instead of fading, however, the red spots turned into two dark-colored square patches on my arm. Nurses thought they might disappear, but they are still resident on my arm over three years later. When I showed one nurse the spots and asked her to please use the paper tape because the other stuff had left me an unwanted souvenir, she exclaimed, "Oh, we *never* use that tape in this department because pretty much everyone is allergic to it!" That might have been nice to know before I ended up with the unrequested tape-made tattoos on my arm.

However, they've grown on me and I've decided I'm thankful for them. Every time I look at my arm, I have a visual reminder of all the amazing things God did through that whole experience. How do you sum up an experience like cancer? You don't, really. So these parallel squares do a good job of symbolizing all that can't be neatly packaged or summed up in a few seconds. They stand for a life-changing event, and I'm glad for them now because they keep me mindful of the fact that I am alive only by God's grace and strength. I need only to glance down at my arm—intentionally or while doing some other task—and I remember why those spots exist and what they symbolize. (Also, I'm glad they're naturally there because I'm not feeling like getting an *actual* tattoo as a reminder.)

Donald Miller talks about going through a challenging event with others and trying to hold the memory of that event alive so as not to lose the meaning or impact of it. He writes,

> I like those scenes in the Bible where God stops people and
> asks them to build an altar. You'd think He was making them

do that for Himself, but I don't think God really gets much from looking at a pile of rocks. Instead, I think God wanted His people to build altars for their sake, something that would help them remember, something they could look back on and remember the time when they were rescued, or they were given grace....We have to make altars.[28]

He has a great point, and when I finished reading that, I had a strong impression that I needed to build an altar to help me remember when I was rescued from the grave. Just as people visit graves and float lanterns ultimately to keep memories alive and not lose the importance of people and events for themselves, God has His followers build altars for their *own* sakes so they don't forget His incredible work in their lives. Abraham, Moses, and many others left altars and wells along their journeys to commemorate what God had done. As Miller points out, it's not like God really needs a pile of rocks for His own gratification. They're really more for the survivors, and He knows that. Whatever shape or form your altar might take, it's probably a better way to keep the memory of such a deeply impactful experience from fading than bringing the topic up in every conversation you have and with every new person you meet, thereby halting all conversation and forever being *that* cancer girl or guy.

At the same time, we still need to tell our stories. There's a reason so many psalmists reference God's miracle of parting the Red Sea and delivering Israel from Egypt (see Psalms 18, 66, 74, 76, 77, 78, 105, 106, 114, 135, and 136). What's interesting is none of those psalmists lived through the incident of the Red Sea. In fact, most of them wrote generations later, during and after captivity. And yet, the psalmists continue coming back to the events of the Red Sea.

These writers' knowledge of the events at the Red Sea came from accounts passed down from generation to generation. If they could go back and point readers to God's amazing works in their ancestors' lives though they weren't even *there*, I think it's probably okay for me to go back and point my friends and family members to God's amazing works in my life through cancer. In fact, I think that's kind of the point. These psalmists aren't living in the past for nostalgia's sake; they're pointing to the life-changing event as if to say, "If God could open up the ocean and let Israel pass through completely unharmed, He is faithful and can surely see us through this trial."

We tell our stories—God's stories in our lives—to encourage and tell the world of His wonders. We build altars to remind ourselves of His faithfulness in our own lives. My altars are the unintended square tattoos on my arm, the picture of me as a baldy on my mirror, and the card in my car with Lamentations 3:19-26 on it:

> I remember my affliction and my wandering, the bitterness and the gall. I well remember them, and my soul is downcast within me. Yet, this I call to mind and therefore I have hope: Because of the Lord's great love, we are not consumed, for His compassions never fail. They are new every morning; great is Your faithfulness. I say to myself, "The Lord is my portion; therefore I will wait for Him." The Lord is good to those whose hope is in Him, to the one who seeks Him; it is good to wait quietly for the salvation of the Lord.

I look at my arm, I remember being bald, and I see this verse when I drive as a way to remember from what depths the Lord rescued me. I remember the pain, the long nights, the anxiety, and the overwhelming scope of the great unknown, but then I call to mind the fact that God in His grace brought me through that fire, that He is good, and that I will wait for Him and trust in His plan.

Maybe your altar is a legitimate tattoo, a bracelet, a keychain, a sticker on your car, a picture in your wallet, a Bible verse on your desk, or an actual pile of rocks, Old Testament style. Whatever you're feeling, I encourage you to build an altar. You don't need to relive all of those harrowing memories every moment of every day, but you don't have to silence people at dinner parties by continually bringing up your experience either. It's okay to move on. After any trial, I think our goal should be to emerge healthier and wiser so we can continue on to face whatever the future holds. But, we need to tell our stories and build altars to remember that God is sovereign, He has a bright hope for our lives, and He even uses cancer and other trials to grow us, impact those around us, and show us His endless wonders.

In the Word:

- **Psalm 40:1-3** "I waited patiently for the Lord; He turned to me and heard my cry. He lifted me out of the slimy pit, out of the mud and mire; He set my feet on a rock and gave me a firm place to stand. He put a new song in my mouth, a hymn of praise to our God. Many will see and fear and put their trust in the Lord."

- **Psalm 56:13** "For You have delivered me from death and my feet from stumbling, that I may walk before God in the light of life."

- **Psalm 77:11** "I will remember the deeds of the Lord; yes, I will remember Your miracles of long ago."

- **Psalm 96:1-3** "Sing to the Lord a new song; sing to the Lord all the earth. Sing to the Lord, praise His name; proclaim His salvation day after day. Declare His glory among the nations, His marvelous deeds among all peoples. For great is the Lord and most worthy of praise; He is to be feared above all gods."

- **Psalm 116:1-2** "I love the Lord, for He heard my voice; He heard my cry for mercy. Because He turned His ear to me, I will call on Him as long as I live."

On the Web:

- Cancer Support Communities (www.cancersupportcommunity. org) hold seminars and events on grief, loss, coping, and survivorship.

- The American Cancer Society (www.cancer.org) has information on survivorship, moving on, and even volunteering to give back under their "Find Support and Treatment" tab. Check out events like Relay for Life to help raise money and awareness for cancer research.

- OncoLink (www.oncolink.org) addresses a variety of topics, with one helpful category titled, "You Survived Cancer...Now What?"

EPILOGUE

Much like with the title of my book, recently my dad asked me another offhand but important question. We were talking about my book and as he thought about my cancer, he looked at me and asked, "What was *that* all about?"

Once again, good question. Though cancer is slowly receding further into my past as the years move on, it's still a part of my life. I'm still under the care of an oncologist, and I still have annual check-ups—in fact, this is something I'll deal with for the rest of my life. Anything out of the ordinary sends me to a doctor these days. I'm much more of a hypochondriac now than I was when Dr. Santi told me he'd be praying for me because I could have something serious. Then, I couldn't fathom something like cancer. Now, a two week long sinus infection sends me to the doctor (though still reluctantly). I don't take chances.

So, what *was* that all about? It all boils down to two truths: God is sovereign, and God has a good plan for our lives.

God is sovereign. When I wonder what the point of something like cancer is, I have to remember that He is sovereign. I like to think of Job, who has a "whatever" theology—one of complete submission to God. It's as if he says, "Whatever you say. It doesn't matter. I'll follow," even if it doesn't look good for the home team—which in his case, it often didn't.

Or think of David in the cave, hiding from Saul and clinging to life. He doesn't give up or decide that he's going to try doing things on his own. He trusts that God is still sovereign.

God is good and has a good plan for our lives. I learned Romans 8:28 in an elementary school musical, and I can still sing you the song today: "And we know that in all things God works for the good of those who love Him, who have been called according to His purpose." I'm not preaching a "health, wealth, and prosperity gospel"; the truth is that our definition of "good" isn't always the same as God's definition of what will truly be best for us. He works everything in our lives for our good and His purpose. Even if we don't always feel or see that right now on earth, He is still good.

I love 1 Corinthians 13:12: "Now we see but a poor reflection as in a mirror; then we shall see face to face. Now I know in part; then I shall know fully, even as I am fully known." We only see in part here on earth—a small glimpse of what is really going on—which means a couple of things. First, we don't have an eternal perspective. But if we pulled the curtain back to see the spiritual realm, I wonder if the "heavenly hosts" would look at us and wonder why we're fighting so hard to stay down here. I wonder if they'd look at us incredulously, saying, "Guys, what are you doing? Why are you clinging to such a broken world when heaven's waiting?"

Secondly, because we see in part, we'll never know who we impact along the journey. As we struggle through highs and lows, we might just be changing others' lives. I still find out about people who've been touched by my story, and that surprises me every time. We can only see in part as we journey, though our impact might be life-changing to many people along the way. I can't, for the life of me, understand why God would use me and that experience, but He does, and that's the mission, isn't it? To love Him and be used by Him.

We simply follow the Lord, Maker of heaven and earth, trusting that He is sovereign and that His plans are good, not knowing who we touch in the process. Since I was in middle school, one of my favorite anthems has been "If You Want Me To" by Ginny Owens, a blind Christian singer and songwriter. It's simple and sweet, but the lyrics have always been strikingly poignant in my walk with the Lord:

> The pathway is broken and the signs are unclear. And I don't know the reason why You've brought me here. But just because You love me the way that You do, I'm gonna walk through the valley if You want me to.

> No I'm not who I was when I took my first step. And I'm clinging to the promise You're not through with me yet. So if all of these trials bring me closer to You, then I will go through the fire if You want me to.

> It may not be the way I would have chosen when You lead me through a world that's not my home. But You never said it would be easy. You only said I'll never go alone.[29]

I've come to the conclusion that I agree with Ginny Owens. It may not be the way I would've chosen when God leads me through crazy times like cancer, but He never said the journey would be easy. The pathway will have cracks and signs that just don't make sense at times. He did promise that He's with us though, and because He loves me enough to sacrifice Himself for me, I'm gonna walk through the valley—or the fire, even—if He wants me to.

I was out on a run a few months ago, and it was two days before the Honolulu Marathon, so lots of runners were scoping out the course. I saw two women running toward me and at first wondered, annoyed, if they were going to scoot over or run me off the sidewalk, until I looked closer. As they came nearer, I noticed that one of the women had a vest on that said "Blind Runner" and the other wore one that said "Guide." I slowed down (and scooted over for them) as they passed me, and I was struck by how cool that was.

Here's a woman who is in good physical shape and wants to run a marathon, but she can't see to complete the race. So, a guide comes along and decides to help her in her task. She does all of the same training as the blind runner, and without her, the woman wouldn't be able to complete the race. I realized how much trust that took on the blind runner's part. She has to just say, "Okay, I believe you," and start moving her legs, having no idea where she's going, what roots or cracks in the sidewalk might be in her path, or even where she needs to turn so that she doesn't smack into objects or other people. This would be disastrous for me. For one, I probably don't trust people that willingly, and secondly, I've tripped and sprawled out enough times with good vision that running with my eyes closed would just be comical.

But, I was struck by what a great picture that is for our lives. We're the blind runners and God's the Guide. He's given us what we need to go through life and complete the course, except for the one small detail that we're completely blind and useless in those abilities without Him to run beside and ahead of us, leading us through the race toward the finish line. He does the important work, but in the end we get a medal and get to show it off to our friends. I want to be like that blind runner—saying, "Okay, God, I trust You. I have no clue where this is leading me, but I know You're sovereign, You are good, and You have good plans for my life, so I'm going to just start running. I may be running blindly, but I know You will guide me along the course."

That's my story at least: running blindly, led by my faithful Guide along an unfamiliar course with minor cracks and roots—and an occasionally giant, seemingly insurmountable hill that somehow I'm over and through before I ever know how or why or what else might be in store in the race that is life. But I know my Guide, and I'm willing to trust Him and just start running.

ACKNOWLEDGEMENTS

Thank you to all of my Kickstarter backers who helped make this book happen! I couldn't have done this without your generosity (and patience!): Lee and Danna Dinkle; Uncle Lorne and Aunt Mary Liechty; Megan Kuehl; the family of Gia and Emmett Berryman; Carol and Gene Pond; Wayne and Karen Copelin; Scott, Karen, and Erica Yaguchi; Scott and Lauri Topping; Jeremy and Stefanie Hansen; Marcus, Susan, and Kimberly Burson; Lori Joiner; Kim and Adrian De La Garza; Bill and Ruth Cunningham; Ashley and Lindsay Foerster; my sister Katie; Jeff, Linda, and Mallory Hinkle; Allison and John Fainter; Dr. Guy and Ellen Fain; Debbie Reitsema; Carrie, Katelynn, Will, and Grant; Kristy and Taylor Bowen; Ruby Whittington; Caroline Hillman; Phyllis and Barry Woodward; Roy Gene Evans; Al Boulden; and Kevin FC and Brenda MC McGinnis. Thanks for believing in my book and in me!

To everyone named in the book: you lived it and there's a reason I included you. Thank you for walking alongside me through that season and for encouraging me. Thanks to all who prayed for and helped me. There are too many of you to list without seeming self-important, but know that I'm sincerely grateful for you and how you carried me through the hardest moments of my life.

Thanks to my HBA ohana for your encouragement and my students (10M!) for committing to buy autographed copies of my book. Thanks to Faye Takushi and Debi Tenney for your editing help and feedback, and thanks to Janice Prager for your encouragement in the process.

Thanks to everyone who helped me with editing, encouragement, and endorsements: Karol Ladd, Ramona Tucker, Aunt Karen, Pete Briscoe, Dr. Gene Wilkes, Joe White, Dr. Gene Pond, Mark Saunders, and Peggy Wehmeyer. Thanks to my WestBow team for your patience and support!

Karen Wright, thanks for your help with my video and for your great support. Becky Ellis, Maile Miller, Tiffany Rawley, and Sarah Spivey: thanks for your encouragement and prayers with this dream!

Caroline, thanks for your unwavering support and encouragement—then and now. Thanks for not freaking out on me at the mall that day and for surviving that crazy Christmas Eve chemo!

Melissa, my CO and my kindred spirit, thanks for being a phone call away and always counseling me through life, through chemo, and through my passions. Thanks for encouraging me to write and keeping my head up when the task became overwhelming.

Thank you to my medical team: Michelle, Sarah, and Dr. Gordon for treating me and physically helping me through this journey. Thank you Dr. Santi for your impeccable timing and prayers. I praise the Lord for all of you!

Thank you to Wheaton College for supporting me in ways I never imagined. Thanks Drs. Lundin, Cohick, Eggiman, and Bacote, and the AHS department for making it possible for me to graduate. Thanks Jen, Channing, Hannah, Maggie, Lo, Kristy and the Hearth House, Rhode, and Harrison for your support. Thanks Kirsten Friedl for all of your help and encouragement. I'm thankful for more acts of love than I can begin to recount from the Wheaton community.

Thanks to my teammates: Stef, Annie, Lisa, Megan, Mal, Kekki, Calla, Leah, Ruth, Jamie, Abby, Emily, Hannah, Smashlie, Kelly, Jenna, Sarah, Brooke, Paige, and Kaitlyn. Thanks for letting me use your names and your stories and for encouraging me that this book would rock. Flabs and Em, I'll get you those royalties someday. You girls are amazing, and I praise God for you. Thanks for helping me kick cancer's...you know.... Thanks to your families for consistently lifting me up as well. I love y'all so much!

Thank you to my second parents, Rick and Lynda Armstrong. Thanks for taking me under your wing and loving me with your words and actions. You are irreplaceable.

Thank you to my family. Thanks for loving me, praying for me, crying with me, offering wisdom and encouragement, and walking through the fire with me. Thanks to the Higginses, Nelsons, McGinnises, MacDinos, Mema and Tutu, the Copelins, the Pursells, the Laynes, Grandmommy Brown, and Grandmommy and Grandaddy. Thanks Mema for being the first person to tell me I was supposed to write. Thank you all for encouraging me to write and imprinting this dream on my heart.

Katie, thanks for answering countless questions about cancer and medical terminology and for believing in me to write this. Madelyn, thanks for contributions of humor and lightheartedness plus your encouragement (sorry it's not in Wake).

Thanks to my mom for taking care of me like when I was a small child. Thanks for letting me growl at you and for just letting it happen. Thanks for rallying the troops and letting me know it was okay to cry and be weak. Thanks for being my biggest fan, greatest help, and strongest advocate with this book. Thanks for your invaluable help in editing and for bearing with me in love when I was impatient or stuck. Thanks to my dad for keeping me so strong. Thanks for encouraging me and rallying your clients to pray for me. Thanks for paying my bills and never complaining about the huge financial impact I caused (especially when it coincided exactly with the recession...). Thank you both for believing in me enough to let me quit my job, crash at home, and write this book. I couldn't have done any of this without y'all.

Most importantly: thank You, Lord, for Your promises, for carrying me through the darkest nights and also the days filled with joy, and for preparing me to walk through the fire and never leaving me. I am here because of You—literally. Thank You for giving me a new song to sing. Thanks for so perfectly reminding me of my purpose in writing every time I doubted it. I will tell of Your mighty acts and wonders all day long.

NOTES

1. Donald Miller, *A Million Miles in a Thousand Years* (Nashville: Thomas Nelson, 2009), 192.

2. "Whisper to Me" written by Warren Barfield. Copyright © New Spring Publishing (ASCAP) / Warren Barfield Music (ASCAP). All rights for the world on behalf of Warren Barfield Music administered by New Spring Publishing. All rights reserved. Used by permission.

3. Warren W. Wiersbe, *Be Worshipful* (Colorado Springs, David C. Cook, 2004), 41.

4. Warren W. Wiersbe, *Be Worshipful* (Colorado Springs, David C. Cook, 2004), 60.

5. Francis Chan, *Crazy Love* (Colorado Springs, David C. Cook, 2008), 146.

6. "Whatever You're Doing (Something Heavenly)" written by Chris Rohman, Dan Gartley, Mark Graalman, Matt Hammitt, Peter Prevost. Copyright © 2008 Birdwing Music (ASCAP) Olde Irish Publishing (BMI) Toledo Tomorrow Music (ASCAP) 1012 Rosedale Music (ASCAP) Eventho Publishing (ASCAP) Look At My Beard (SESAC) Stonebrook Music Company (SESAC) River Oaks Music Company (BMI) (adm. at EMICMGPublishing.com) All rights reserved. Used by permission.

7. "Closer" written by Warren Barfield. Copyright © New Spring Publishing (ASCAP) / Warren Barfield Music (ASCAP). All rights for the world on behalf of Warren Barfield Music administered by New Spring Publishing. All rights reserved. Used by permission.

8. Donald Miller, *A Million Miles in a Thousand Years* (Nashville, Thomas Nelson, 2009), 195-6.

9. Robin Eisner, "Men Spend $1 Billion Yearly Fighting Baldness" (New York: ABC News, 14 February 2012).

10. "Your Love Oh Lord" written by Brad Avery, David Carr, Mac Powell, Mark D. Lee, Samuel Tai Anderson. Copyright © 1999 Vandura 2500 Songs (ASCAP) (adm. at EMICMGPublishing.com) / New Spring Publishing (ASCAP) All rights reserved. Used by permission.

11. Henry James, *The Bostonians* (New York: Barnes and Noble Classics, 2005), 378.

12. Warren W. Wiersbe, *Be Worshipful* (Colorado Springs: David C. Cook, 2004), 236.

13. Elisabeth Elliot, *Through Gates of Splendor* (Carol Stream: Tyndale, 2005), 263.

14. "God is God" written by Steven Curtis Chapman 2. Copyright © 2001 Sparrow Song (BMI) (adm. at EMICMGPublishing.com) / Peach Hill Songs (BMI) All rights reserved. Used by permission.

15. "Whom Have I But You" written by David Ruis. Copyright © 1996 Mercy/Vineyard Publishing (ASCAP) & Vineyard Songs (Canada) (SOCAN) Admin. in North America by Music Services o/b/o Vineyard Music USA. All rights reserved. Used by permission.

16. Robert J. Morgan, *The Red Sea Rules, 10 God-Given Strategies for Difficult Times* (Nashville: Thomas Nelson, 2001), 6.

17. Ron Hall and Denver Moore, *Same Kind of Different as Me* (Nashville: Thomas Nelson, 2006), 230-1.

18. Scott Hamilton, *The Great Eight: How to be Happy (Even When You Have Every Reason to be Miserable)* (Nashville: Thomas Nelson, 2009).

19. Warren W. Wiersbe, *Be Worshipful* (Colorado Springs: David C. Cook, 2004), 40.

20. Warren W. Wiersbe, *Be Worshipful* (Colorado Springs: David C. Cook, 2004), 55.

21. Jim Dailey, "Preparing for Eternity—On Purpose: A Conversation with Rick Warren," *Decision Magazine* (Billy Graham Evangelistic Association, 1 November 2004).

22. *NIV Study Bible*, commentary on Psalm 9:1 (Grand Rapids: Zondervan, 2002).

23. A sermon delivered on Sunday morning, June 6, 1869, by C. H. Spurgeon, at The Metropolitan Tabernacle, Newington.

24. Judith Viorst, *Alexander and the Terrible, Horrible, No Good, Very Bad Day* (New York: Atheneum, 1972).

25. Donald Miller, *A Million Miles in a Thousand Years* (Nashville: Thomas Nelson, 2009), 179, 182.

26. James R. Hansen, *First Man: The Life of Neil A. Armstrong* (New York: Simon & Schuster, 2005), 371-2.

27. "Blessed be Your Name" written by Beth Redman, Matt Redman. Copyright © 2002 Thankyou Music (PRS) (adm. worldwide at EMICMGPublishing.com excluding Europe which is adm. by Kingswaysongs) All rights reserved. Used by permission.

28. Donald Miller, *A Million Miles in a Thousand Years* (Nashville: Thomas Nelson, 2009), 213-4.

29. "If You Want Me To" written by Ginny Owens, Kyle Matthews. Copyright © 1999 Universal Music - Brentwood Benson Publishing (ASCAP). All rights reserved. Used by permission.

CPSIA information can be obtained at www.ICGtesting.com
Printed in the USA
LVOW13s1247171213

365588LV00001B/106/P